August in America

By

August Summer

Mama and Me

'I've always been a big girl. Mama says that's why I'm an only child. Says after my big head pushed through her tiny privates she knew right then and there that she was now a firm believer in abortion. It's funny though. It never bothered me that I was an only child and never had any brothers or sisters. I think the reason why was because mama had three jobs. She worked part-time when she felt like it, went to school a lot and took care of me.

I was her first job and she spent every spare minute taking care of me, teaching me all the finer points in life and raising me to be a lady. Mama adored her baby girl and catered to my every wish and desire. If you ask me that's what kids are missing nowadays someone who makes them a priority. I was mama's priority.

Mama didn't always have real good luck with men because she was too darn smart and independent. I think she intimidated most of the men that came-a-calling. If she didn't intimidate them she made it plain that if they wanted her it was a package deal and I came along. I think this scared a lot of them away but it never seemed to bother her that she didn't have a man. She had me and that was all that counted in her eyes. She along with my grandfather's help made sure she had everything she could possibly want.

That's not to say that we were rich or anything. Mama didn't necessarily need money to be happy. She had a wealth of knowledge and liked the simple things in life. Like it

wasn't nothing for her to get on her laptop and find a new recipe then fix it even better than the chef that originally created it. When she'd finished creating and adding her own special flair to it and we'd eaten, she'd grab a bottle of wine, a glass, turn on some of that horrible smooth jazz that she was so fond of and pick up whatever she was reading on that particular day head for the parlor where she'd sit in her favorite recliner in front of the fireplace and wile the hours away reading. This sort of thing was heaven to mama who had also been an only child and the apple of her daddy's eye so the absence of a man didn't bother her in the least. She was used to being alone—well that is where men were concerned—and still never had enough time so consumed was she with me and her own little projects. She was what you would call rich in spirit.

To tell you the truth I admired her. She was a free spirit if I ever saw one. She would read and dream and if something really affected her in a big way she'd either confront it head on or write about it. Oh, the woman could write and from a very early age she inspired me to do the same. Well, perhaps inspire me may be too loose a term. What she did was force me to write something in my journal each and every night. When I was about thirteen or fourteen she didn't have to force me anymore. By then it had become habit. It was like therapy. If something would happen in school and I didn't want to discuss it with mama I'd write it down and for some reason putting my thoughts on paper would help me to see the whole incident that much clearer. It would also help

when something was really and truly bothering me. I guess mama knew this would be an outlet for me one day and that's why she made such a fuss about me keeping a daily journal. And it really has been.

I grew up in Hollis, Queens in a tight little community where folks—Black folks mostly—bought their first homes. I think they call them starter homes. But for most of them this was the start and the finish.

Most of them had moved out here from the inner city and took pride in their homes. Most were young couples just starting out with their families so most of us were kids who grew up together and we were more like a family than just a neighborhood. I mean mama would go outside to watch us play and if there were no other adults outside she would just naturally be the one who would assume the role of parent. That's the way I grew up and it was great. We all got along well and if something bad happened in the neighborhood like it did when Ms. Reeves died the whole block would come out to share the good times they had when Ms. Reeves was alive and in grieving her passing. That's just how it was. There was no ADHD or pedophilia back then. There were no school shootings. That's not to say there weren't shootings and stabbings but they were few and far between. Not like today.

And then my world came to an end. We moved to Jersey. Mama got a job teaching school at one of the community colleges over in Jersey City so we moved. And for the first time in my life I hated mama but she said it was for the best and I guess she had a right to want to realize her own dreams and that may all have been true but I hated her just the same.

All I knew is she was tearing me away from my friends, from the warmth of my block, my security blanket. I was moving somewhere strange, somewhere foreign; somewhere I didn't know a soul. I thought my life had ended. Jersey was like some distant land like Egypt or China.

Like most New Yorkers I had the attitude that there was New York—God's gift to mankind—and then there was everyplace else which was nowhere in my eyes. That's how I saw it and I think most New Yorker's shared the same feelings. We're an arrogant group. But there's a lot of truth about our attitude. When you're competing against and trying to shine with eight million other people in a space the size of Manhattan or Brooklyn you'd better be good. I think Frank Sinatra or somebody said it best when they said if you can make it there you can make it anywhere. In my eyes like most New Yorkers there is no place like it.

Anyway we moved to this foreign land called Jersey and I hated it. The people seemed so different. They just weren't cool. New Yorkers had a certain kind of swagger about them. It was in everything they did. The way they walked. The way they talked. The way they thought about things. I enrolled in high school a few days later and immediately became the butt of jokes.

For the first time in my life I was the new kid on the block and I didn't like it. They started off with the fat jokes. 'What's the bus driver say when Wanda Sherman gets on the bus?' Someone would invariably say, 'Two fares buddy,' at which time they would all break out in laughter. This went on for the first couple of weeks. Then one day I went to the gym to shoot around down at the far end of the court where no one was. And being that there was a game going on at the other end I went pretty much unnoticed. The game was pretty intense and caught my attention and I must have caught theirs too cause when one of them went down with an ankle sprain I heard my name for the first time from someone other than a teacher.

"Yo Wanda you wanna play?"

I knew I could run with these Jersey clowns and I was determined to show them that I was no one to be played with. It didn't matter who guarded me. I torched them. My shot was on. I guess you could say I was in the zone. If they guarded me tight on the

outside I took 'em to the hole. If they laid off me on the perimeter I reined threes on them like Steph Curry. When it was all over it was like I was reborn. Well, at least I was in their eyes. No longer was I just the 'big girl'.

"Yo, Sherman where did you learn to hoop like that?" One brother on the St. Anthony's squad asked. "Coach Hurley would love to look you over if you've got some time." I smiled but declined the invitation.

"You got skills girl," another said in passing but there was one young brother who'd been watching me the whole time who refused to say anything. I could feel his eyes on me. When the game was over he came over to me picked up my sweat suit and handed it to me.

"You live over by the Waterfront don't you?"

"I do. Why do you ask?"

"We take the same bus. I live over there too. You heading home?"

"Yes."

"Mind if I walk you. My name's Brody. Well, actually my name is Terrance but everyone calls me Brody."

"Nice to meet you Terrance. I'm…"

"Wanda. I know," he said smiling. "C'mon let's get outta here."

That was three weeks ago. I guess you can say he was enamored or something. I don't know but he made himself a fixture in my life. He called, picked me up from school, waited for me after school and to tell you the truth I kinda liked all the attention. He was cute too in his own sorta way. And although most of my friends had been males in Queens this was somehow different. And then one day as we were getting off the bus he grabbed my hand as we got off the bus. At first I was shocked and felt awkward and my first instinct was to pull away but for some reason I didn't. Actually it felt good in a weird sort of way. We walked like this for the two blocks 'til we reached my house. By the time he let go for me to get the keys out of my book bag I was soaking wet. I don't know why but I was. When I got in the house I just fell out on the coach. When mama got home an hour later I was still there.

"Is my baby alright?" she said smiling.

"Couldn't be better," I said smiling back.

"Jersey's growing on you I see? Daddy was worried about you adjusting. I assured him that children are even more adaptable than adults. And my Wanda would adapt to her new surroundings in time. Just didn't think it would be this quickly," she said smiling. And I knew mama knew.

Life and Death

It was a typical July evening in Bartow County, Georgia. The sun had gone down for now but it was still a smothering ninety six degrees in the shade; the kind of heat that simply drained you and left you dripping wet even if you were sitting still.

Mamie, and Beulah and I were accustomed to this and sat outside my little one room cabin on Master Jennings place. The little thatch roofed hut I had was made mainly of bamboo stalks bound loosely together with hemp.

When I first came to the Jennings in November—oh some five or six years ago, I can't rightly recall—I told some of the men that were constructing my little hut that there were openings in the bamboo and I valued my privacy. They just smiled at me and said 'Miss June when July comes around you gonna wish those tiny slats were even bigger than they were now'. And you know what? They ain't never lied.

Most of the time I wear a head rag. For y'all that don't know that's just a old piece of rag that I ties around my head to keep my hair up off my neck and outta my eyes. And in the evening when I take it off I can actually ring it out and Lord knows I can get a half a cup of water or sweat when I do this.

When I was first brought here I believe I was no more than about twenty and all

them little fresh boys used to hide outside and wait 'til I disrobed at night and come peek

through the opening in them slats but once they got an eyeful and memorized what I

looked like naked they stopped but it got so hot here in the summer months that I got

used to sleeping in the nude and I could care less who saw me. It was just that hot.

Lot of things done changed since I first got here though. Them boys that was so

curious when I first got here have lost interest or moved onto other things nowadays.

And no longer do I work in the big house which is what I was first brought here to do.

No. I guess missy thought I had a little too much attitude and was a little too belligerent

so she had me put out in da fields. And even though this Georgia sun is somethin' to be

mindful of I much prefers it to workin' in da big house where's I got to yassuh' dem

white folks all day. Sometimes I be out dere and I got my bonnet and head rag on and I

jes forgets that mean ol' spiteful sun and jes drift off into a world of my own.

It's a world where there ain't no slavery or mean ol' white folks always telling

you what to do. It's a world of green pastures and fast rushing streams where I sit and

watch the clear blue waters rush over my feet. I likes to gets lost in these thoughts.

But today I'm pretty content to just sit outside my little hut after a long hard day

in da fields with my two best friends Beulah and Mamie.

Beulah's a little older than Mamie and me. And if I would gather to guess I'd say she's in her mid to late thirties whereas me and Mamie be in our late twenties. These is all approximations 'cause ain't no one ever write down when us niggras was born. Anyway, Beaulah is older and one beautiful woman. You can tell she mixed 'cause her hair is straight as a peacock's feather. She say she a little on the heavy side but the mens don't seem to think so. And they all the time flirtin' with her and trying to get her to do things she say she ain't got no interest in.

Now Mamie she's a lot like me. We agrees on most everything and especially when it comes to menfolk. I guess you could say we both attractive but no men talk to us at all. They all say we mean as rattlesnakes but we agree that we ain't got no time for no men. Truth is and I don't think Mamie will ever admit it. I know I won't. But the truth of the matter is I think we'd both love to have a man and fall in love and have a bunch of screamin' younguns runnin' 'round but just not the way things be at the present moment.

I seen too many instances of just that sort of thing and then the next thing you know white folks hit a rough patch and wind up selling a husband or wife off and maybe the kids' jes like it ain't nothing. And I jes ain't got that to do.

As it is the only family I got is Mamie and Beulah and ain't neither of them related to me by blood. So, when the mens come a pushin' up and talkin' 'bout courtin' and the like I jes tells 'em to 'Go on! Git!' Nowadays they just like dem boys that useta come 'round. They done lost their curiosity.

Still, ain't nothin' better than seein' young love. Me. Well I guess I've just gotten too durn old to weather another heartbreak so I just watch and smile and wish 'em all the best in the world. Like Pecolia and Fred. Pecolia can't be more than seventeen or

eighteen and she the cutest, little thang. She's mocha brown—sorta like coffee with just a tad too much cream—with two cute braids running down the back of her head. She been wearing that same hairstyle since she was ten or eleven. And even though it ain't the most becoming hairstyle and we all agree that she could do a lil more than those two braids Fred seems to like them nonetheless.

Now Fred is as big as Pecolia is tiny and me and Beulah alla time laughin' about how Pecolia just may have a change of heart when it comes time to consummate their union.

Oh, Pecolia's a virgin and let me tell you how I know. First of all, she stay in prayer meeting every minute she ain't with Fred. Mamie say she stay in prayer meeting praying to da good Lord to show her the true spirit so she don't drop dem drawers every time Fred—wit' his good lookin' self—approaches her.

I don't know about that but the other reason I knowed she was a virgin was that her pappy keeps a tight rein on her lil fast tail and makes sho' she in before the sun goes down. 'Sides that her legs is tight and what I mean by that is when a gal done had a man or two up in her what I likes to refer to as 'her more than precious' you'll usually see a gap between her legs. But ain't no gap between Pecolia's thighs. No siree. She a sho'nuff virgin.

But that don't much mean nothin'. I mean I'm sho they both gets hot and bothered from time-to-time. That's just human nature when you be in love. And sometime it just be the nature of things regardless of bein' in love or not. It even happens to me from time-to-time.

But theirs is more than that. Soon as Panowski, the ovaseer let's us go in da evening Pecolia and Fred meet at the ol' oak tree up by the big house. Every night they meet there. It don't matter if it's raining cats and dogs or the middle of winter and cold as the dickens they wait for each other and walk home every night hand-in-hand.

Half the time you can walk by and speak and they'll nod but they ain't really seen you. They cain't see nothin' but each other. And I ain't never seen 'em pass a cross word between 'em. All they do is talk and smile and laugh at each other with them goo goo eyes that say 'you're the one that's meant for me'. It's all the time like they in their own little world and no one or nothing else exists. And it's truly a beautiful thing to see especially in this awful world of misery called slavery.

Still, Mamie and I who are all too often embroiled in this or that agree on one thing. Ain't no way it would be us.

But Beulah sees it different. She says she'd give it all up for one day of being hopelessly in love to which I say 'if that's the case why don't you go ahead and do it. You certainly have enough men calling on you every day not to be wishing and hopin'.

"Baby gal, there's a big difference between a man tryin' to poke my fine brown frame and possessin' it."

"I know that's right."

"Look here they come now. And always hand-in-hand. He sho' ain't tryna hide where his heart and soul is."

"Sho' ain't."

"That niggras in love."

"She ain't turnin' her head either. She cain't see no one but him."

"If I was five years younger I believe I'd give ol' gal a run for her money. I'd turn his head and when he looked in my direction I'd make sho' he never looked back. I'd throw this thang on his fine ass and sho' him what real bondage was. I'd take my good luck charm and lock him down for the rest of his born days. This here slavery wouldn't be nothin' to the shackles I'd put on him," Mamie said laughing.

"You'd take that chile's man Mamie?" Beulah asked grinning widely.

"Somebody going to sooner or later. A kiss on the cheek and a pretty smile ain't gonna cut it but for so long. There's more than you and me that got that strong throbbing between our legs and he sho nuff could ease that noise."

"I know that's the truth," Beulah said laughing. "It's been so long I got cob webs on top of rust."

"You two are disgraceful. And supposed to be Christian womans."

"Trust me the good Lord fully understands my needs."

It wasn't long after that Pecolia and Fred announced their plans to marry. And never were two souls happier. We all speculated on whether Fred had finally gotten the best of Pecolia and she was pregnant but after several months and her not showing we just figured that Fred had grown tired of waiting and decided the only way to have her fully was to take her hand in marriage.

Mamie and Beulah had been asked to make the wedding dress since they were the best seamstresses. And I was to make the wedding cake. Everything seemed set for the wedding when three days before the wedding a large, burly old white man pulled up in front of the big house where Pecolia stood in her usual spot in front of the old oak tree. It was quitting time and she paid little mind to the white man, the sheriff and massa arguing. After all, she had a long time ago learned that white folks affairs was none a hers.

Yet, the voices grew and she couldn't help but hear the man shouting at massa about some unpaid debt as the sheriff did his best to intervene and come to some viable solution. When it was finally made clear to both the sheriff and the man that massa could

not pay his debt the man decided to settle on the next best thing. He decided he'd take five of massa's top hands instead. Looking hastily around he grabbed four healthy bucks now coming up from the lower forty.

"And give me that there gal standing there by that old oak. She looks like she could make a handy bed warmer come winter."

Massa had little choice but to agree being that he owed the man a right tidy sum of money and the man drove off with the five slaves shackled to the buckboard one of which was Pecolia.

When Fred arrived some five or ten minutes later and didn't find his smiling Pecolia and wife to be waiting for him they said he darn near lost his mind. When he was told what had happened to his darling Pecolia they say he went straight up to massa and demanded he return his fiancée to him. I guess you know that massa had him whipped for being disrespectful and belligerent and it was days before Fred was able to move following the whipping. Most of us believed he just plain lost his will to live which is why it took a big strong buck like him so long to recuperate. When he did he just wasn't the same ol' Fred. Mamie said she felt so bad for the po' boy she broke down and offered herself to him but he declined.

In a few days when all seemed to be back to normal two lil younguns came a runnin' into the quarters shouting about some man being down by the creek where they were fishin'. Well, there were always one or two men down by the creek fishin' or wilin' away the time when they had off so we thought nothin' of it but bein' that it was Saturday evenin' and we no longer had a wedding to prepare for we followed the younguns down to the creek. And there we found Fred swingin' from that ol' weepin' willow.

Like Samson and Delilah

"You ready babe," Samson said as he grabbed his keys off the table by the front door.

He really hadn't wanted to go but had agreed after much nagging and debate. In the end he asked as he always did why he even bothered. The results were always the same as he checked the knot in his tie in front of the mirror.

"Two minutes," Delilah shouted from the bathroom.

Another meet and greet, Samson thought to himself. With a position as director of one of the largest growing Black owned hair products companies in the U.S. Delilah already had too much on her plate but ever since he'd known her she had this insatiable desire to network and be out there in the limelight. The spotlight had never appealed to him. She called it networking and he wondered who it was that she needed to meet. He could remember the conversation they'd had so many times in the past.

"Samson. Come on. You can sell your books out there. And you know Najee's performing."

I could give less than a fuck who was performing and although I loved jazz Najee was not at the top of the list of performers I wanted to see.

"Besides you're always complaining about never getting out or going out. Here's not only a chance to get out but a chance to network as well."

I had to wonder if she was just naive or slow as well.

"Tell me something D? Who helped you get started?"

"Started with what?"

"With your hair care business?"

"No one. It was just an idea I had when all of my sorority sisters were always complaining about their hair anytime we were going out. And me being a chemistry major I just sought an answer to their questions and I guess Black women's problems in general."

"I understand that. What I'm asking is how you came up with a marketing strategy and found distribution for your products and who helped you?"

"I can't say that anyone really helped me. Aside from you I can't really think of anybody. You remember those days. It wasn't easy."

"And you're telling me that today and after all the work we put in trying to get your company off the ground that you would offer someone the secret to your success just because?"

"Hell no. Putting in the work makes the joy of your success that much sweeter. And I truly believe that many of us are simply lacking the perseverance and drive. I think that's the main difference between failure and success in an undertaking."

"I hear you and agree completely. But what I'm asking you is would you tell others the secret to your success?"

"Absolutely."

"So tell me again. I don't think I understand."

"It's called perseverance and drive along with the help and support of a loving mate," Delilah said smiling and kissing me on my forehead.

"So you wouldn't give them any detailed help or financial sponsoring in their attempts to reach the level you have?"

Delilah laughed.

"They have the same twenty four hours in a day that I have."

"I hear you."

"It just depends on how bad you want it. Most folks say they want it—meaning success—but aren't willing to back up what they want with the effort it takes to achieve

it. So, and until they put forth the effort I can't help them. You know the time and effort we put in trying to get Our Roots off the ground. How many long sleepless nights did we have to endure?"

"Trust me. I do remember. And you believe that by going to this affair or what you call networking that the CEO's of these corporations are going to share the details of their success with you a stranger? And you're going to spend fifty dollars on a booth with the hope that someone is going to pick you out of the thousands of people there to share with you the secrets of his empire?"

"You know what Samson? If you're so opposed to going out and meeting a better class of people then you don't have to go," she said. She was annoyed and it was obvious.

I loaded some books from my library as well as a few I'd written and one she'd recently published and filled the trunk then resumed my seat in the library where I continued working on my latest novel which would sustain me though I didn't like it in the least.

A few minutes later Delilah entered the library and I was at once angry for being tired and not wanting to go. Delilah wore the brand new blue and white Liz Claiborne blouse with the back out that she'd begged me for and her new blue and white opened toed pumps. My heart raced. And I realized what had initially attracted me to her.

My pride would not allow me to change my mind and I refused to give in to the feelings of jealousy that were now invading my personal space. What if someone else recognized the beauty that I now saw? I probably knew men as well—if not better—than I knew women. No, there was no mistake about that at all. In my eyes men were logical. Women' on the other hand moved recklessly guided by emotions ad whims. And I knew that the beauty I now saw was not limited to my eyes alone. There would be men there that saw and would be enamored just as I was.

"You sure you won't change your mind about joining me?" She asked making sure that I saw her in all her finery.

"No babe. You look especially nice. I'm loving the blouse," hating it as I said it. The back and shoulders were out exposing way too much flesh."

"You really like it? You don't think it's too revealing?"

"Not in the least. What it is is sexy as hell," I said never lying and wishing she'd wear something else. "You go ahead and enjoy yourself. I'll pass this time." I said trying hard as hell to remain cool and not let my jealousy show through as I remembered something I'd read awhile ago. 'You cannot possess another person. When it's time for them to go you must simply resign yourself to the fact that there is a reason for the seasons and all you can do is enjoy them while they're present. I'd always used this as

my mantra for my relationships.

In order to further safeguard my heart from the hurt that often accompanies relationships I made it a point to never restrict myself to one woman. My son used to tell me that he could never settle for a piece of apple pie when there so many different flavors. On one day he might have a taste for key lime, the next day his palate wanted lemon meringue and on the third day he may very well have a taste for pumpkin or blueberry each with its own distinct taste.

I understood—well that was—up until Delilah entered the picture. Now my world evolved around her and I'd done something I promised never to do. I married her.

She left that evening and my discomfort increased with each hour that she was gone but I refused to call her. I would mask my jealous insecurities and pretend to have faith. I considered myself good. I'd come to an easy place in my life after having had to traverse some pitfalls that I brought into my life. I had endured and overcome and at fifty I'd come to an easy peace. I had just come to like myself again and in my solitude had all but eliminated most of the negative forces always ready to disrupt the tranquility I'd now come to know. I was still a work in progress but I was focused and had some direction. If there was anything I still wrestled with it was Delilah. Sure I loved her. She meant the world to me but she had not found the solace I'd come to know. It was disheartening to me but there was little I could do. My father used to tell me that everyone finds peace in their own time and I only prayed that Delilah would soon find her God.

Three hours later I heard the front door open as I lay in bed watching something or another on TV.

"How did it go?" I asked.

"It was nice. The vice president of Coca Cola was there and a few other power players were there. I got a chance to meet them as well as Najee. He was really good. I think you would have enjoyed him."

"You sell any books?"

"I sold three of yours."

"Did you sell any of yours?"

"No," she said handing me twenty five or thirty dollars.

I had to admit I was relieved that there wasn't more to tell and let it go at that. I thought it a valuable experience but a few months later when she approached me around attending a similar venue I was a little exasperated. I didn't have money to keep contributing to whoever it was that approached her with a get rich quick scheme that preyed on up-and-coming Black entrepreneurs like her.

"Ralph's having another fair for up-and-coming entrepreneurs. We should go."

"How much is it?"

"It's fifty dollars a booth but more than that it's a chance for you to get your books out there and get some exposure and network."

"How much did you make last time?"

"You know how much I made last time."

"Yes I do and it seems to me that the only person profiting off of these fairs is the person renting the booths. He doesn't advertise. All he's really interested in is the booth rental."

"Well, I'm just going to support the building fund and I'd really like for you to join me," she said.

I agreed just because it was easier than having this discussion all over again. She was not going to see the light. Throwing on a pair of navy blue Dockers, a white polo shirt and some penny loafers I packed the trunk and we headed off to support Ralph and the building fund.

Four hours later, I turned to her.

"You ready to go?" I asked.

"When you are."

I loaded the car. There was no need to say anything. In the four hours we'd been there we may have seen three people and not sold a book or met anyone of note. I was angry but tried my best to remain congenial. I had no time to waste and it was obvious that I had just been suckered by another one of Ralph's schemes. Now I don't know what type of hold he had over Delilah but it just seemed like common sense that no one was giving away anything and she had been duped again. But I loved her and so I supported her in this latest fiasco. I only hoped that she had on her second venture taken one of life's lessons from it. Now I am in no way famous but there are few men I look up to or idolize. There are a few men throughout history that I do respect and idolize and I'm sure if I get to naming them they will seem obvious and mundane so I will not mention them

but there are few men that I aspire to be solely because of their wealth. Intellect is what inspires me and I find few men in this world of mediocrity that are awe inspiring. That is not to say that they don't exist. It could be that I'm simply out of the loop. Still, I believe that this quest to rub noses with the rich and famous does not inspire me. For me it just seems an easier voyage to travel vicariously and pick up a book about someone recognized for his accolades which brings me to Alexis DeTocqueville, Machiavelli and persons such as Thoreau but to go out randomly hoping that someone you bump into is going to both enlighten you and inspire seems but a random chance.

I loved her but I guess our age difference and motivation didn't equate to us meeting on the same moral or intellectual plane. Still, I did everything to support her sporadic and whimsical pleas.

She was off on another one of her jaunts to link up with whatever it was that was going to turn her meteoric rise into a supernova while I plodded on trying to make ends meet through a formula which incorporated hard work and the idea that persistence overcomes resistance.

And then one day following another night out networking she arrived home. I'd grown accustomed to being home alone.

"How did it go?" I queried the way any good husband would do glad she was home and in my company again.

"It was good bay but we need to talk," she said as she changed into her night gown.

"Concerning?"

"I don't think this is working. I met this guy tonight. It's nothing serious or anything but I want you to move out. I want a divorce."

I was devastated. So this was the power of networking. I understood now.

Lil Junior Parker

Everybody useta call him Lil Junior Parker on account of that's all he useta listen to. His real name was Matthew but I think I'm the onliest one that knew that. To everybody else he was Lil Junior Parker. I known him ever since I can remember. I think my earliest remembrances was in Miss DeWitt's class in Pre-K. He was bad even back then and if it was one thing I knew back then it was that I was going to marry Lil Junior Parker. Mama didn't think it was such a good idea at the time on account I was only four or five but even then I knew what I wanted and I wanted Lil Junior Parker even if he never even knew I existed.

By the time we hit second grade I let everybody know that he was my man. But you know there's always someone out there that don't believe you and wanna try you and this was no different. Her name was Thelma Louise and she was a cute lil' girl. She wasn't quite as cute as me and mama kept me dressed but she was cute just the same. And when school would let out the girls would walk with the girls and the boys would walk with the boys. Well, that's what most of us would do but Thelma Louise somehow saw fit to try to tag along with Lil Junior Parker and his boys. At first I looked at it

innocent enough and figured that she was just exchanging homework or something on account that she missed a lotta days 'cause her mama worked all the time forcing her to stay home and mind her younger brothers and sisters. But no this went on for more than a week and it wasn't that I had anything against Thelma Louise or nothing like that but everybody knew that the boys walked with the boys and the girls walked with the girls. Everybody knew that. Everybody but Thelma Louise. But to be honest she knew but she just didn't care.

At first, I didn't know what her intentions were but the more I saw her walking with them boys the more clearer it came to me that she was interested in my Lil Junior Parker so I knew that if I had any plans for Lil Junior Parker I was gonna have to step in now and shut this little, fast, hussy down. And so with my girls behind I walked up to Thelma Louise.

"Thelma Louise you know the rules," I said. I wasn't mad or nothing and like I said I liked Thelma Louise.

"What you talkin' about Gina?"

"You know the rules Thelma. The girls walk with the girls."

"Maybe I don't wanna walk with the girls Gina."

"It's the rules."

"If Lil Junior Parker wasn't with them boys I bet you wouldn't mind half so much."

"You right. Everybody in school knows that Lil Junior Parker is my man and I don't want you no where's near him you little bitch," I shouted.

Lil Junior Parker just stood there with his mouth open. He knew better than to say anything or I woulda whooped him the same way I was going to whoop Thelma Louise. And she knew too but she had to save face and so she started to say something and then everything became a blur. I think she said 'you can't tell me what to do Gina'. And the next think I knew I had both her pigtails in one hand and was gnawing on her arm pretty good when Ms. Hatchet pulled me off a her.

When I got up there was a crowd so I made sure that everyone knew the rules.

"And the same thing's gonna happen to any of you that messes with my man."

When I got home that day mama looked at me. I had dirt in my hair and my dress was torn in two or three places but all she said was…

"Did you handle your business dear?"

That was fifty two years ago. Me and Lil Junior Parker been married near sixty years now and to this day he ain't never looked at another woman nor they look at him. They knows the rules..

Musings from a Misguided Militant

A couple of days ago I completed Mumia Abu Jamal's book <u>Live from Death Row</u> and although I found it quite a compelling read I nonetheless found myself somewhat detached compartmentalizing his pain and filing it among the compassionate empathy and apathy file long reserved for the survival of African American men in America.

Putting it away as just another tragic plight in the long list of historical tragedies of Black men in America I turned on the television and flicked from Hang 'Em High with Clint Eastwood to CNN where the continuing murder saga of Michael Brown continues to unfold. Is there any question of injustice in America when an eighteen year old Black man fleeing from a white police officer is shot six times? Yes. He was fleeing. And yet I like most other Blacks who have grown up in urban areas know that when the police report eventually comes out it is the white cop whose civil rights will have been violated.

In most cases, there will be the discrediting of eyewitnesses and the collusion and corroboration of the police account will happen a few days after the actual event has taken place. This is standard procedure and can be presented to the general public after all the facts (or lies), are in. In most cases this can take one of three classic scenarios. The victim who will soon be discredited through classic character assassination will either be said to have been possessing a shiny object, in a drug crazed stupor or in Michael Brown's case a thug and hoodlum with a long criminal background who has perpetrated some heinous crime such as stealing a handful of cigars, (with an estimated value of forty dollars), therefore constituting the right to be murdered in broad daylight in the street before countless witnesses. How often have we heard this? Such a brazen act of murder only exhibits the utter disdain by those in positions of authority have for Black men in America.

Almost every year of my life I've seen or read about it in one of New York tabloids. It happened with the same regularity as the Fourth of July. And after awhile your reactions become slower, duller, more callous and insensitive. You become cold, bitter and the enemy is clearly defined. The enemy becomes the very same ones that are supposedly there to protect and serve you.

When defended by the media and others who set up trust funds for the suspended officer it makes a rather clear statement and that statement is that the murder and beating of Black men is not only condoned but advocated.

When I meet strangers, (most of whom are people of color), like myself and tell them my age, (I am fifty six), eyebrows raise, not because I have a youthful demeanor but because it is unusual, somewhat rare in fact for a Black man to reach this milestone somewhat intact. To not have a criminal record or some other variance of abnormality according to society's cultural norms is in and of itself an abnormality for a Black man in America. But that is not to say that I like many of my Black brothers has gone unscathed by this racist regime that is America.

My father, now deceased graduated from New York University. He went on to receive his Masters degree from Columbia University and later received his doctorate degree. Later he taught English at Columbia University's Teacher's College. He went on to author several books which were used in the New York City school system.

I, on the other hand, after graduating high school wasn't immediately inclined to follow in my father's footsteps and chose instead to serve my country. I joined the United States Marine Corps the day after the Fourth of July still in search of my own freedom and independence. I was sent to Parris Island, South Carolina where I was called everything from a libba lipped jigaboo to a nigga jig porch monkey and when bored simply nigga by my white drill instructors. I had long ago grown accustomed to racism having gone to an all-white Catholic school where I was the only Black male for twelve years in a rapidly changing Queens neighborhood during the formative years of integration. So, these tactics bothered me little.

Leaving Parris Island I went to Camp Lejeune in Jacksonville, North Carolina and encountered much the same treatment. One night in particular, however stands out. A few of my buddies went out to Jacksonville for a night on the town after spending two weeks in the field. On our return to base the M.P.'s stopped the cab which my friends and I were in to check I.D.'s an unusual occurrence and especially since they didn't check the white cab driver's I.D. I, however, in a rush and always running late had forgotten my wallet and when I couldn't produce mine I was immediately taken from the cab and placed under arrest.

Now having undergone the routine at different junctures of my life for such things as walking while Black, smiling while Black, staring at a policeman while Black... I was accustomed to this too and so I did as ordered and climbed quietly into the jeep with the M.P. He immediately took out his .45 and pointed it at my head and proceeded to drive with one hand on the wheel and one hand pointing his gun at me. I, of course, knew my place and did the only thing a person in my place could do.

I prayed.

Being handcuffed and having a gun pointed at my head was a new occurrence and lowering my voice almost to a whisper so as not to sound threatening or be charged with resisting arrest. I said. 'Excuse me officer, can you tell me what I did?'

Through hate filled eyes, he glanced at me and I wondered how this young man not much older than me could be filled with so much hatred towards someone he'd never met before but then it came to me. This was the disease best known and afflicting countless white Americans. More deadlier than the combination of Aids, cancer and Ebola it plagues and threatens to be the death of all America. He was afflicted with racism.

And due to racism in his eyes he'd met me countless times. He saw me when he saw Martin stirring up the masses. He saw me when he saw Malcolm X cry for us to defend ourselves. He saw me when he saw Muhammad Ali beat Gerry Cooney and Oscar Bonavena to bloody pulps. And he saw me when he saw Jackie Robinson singlehandedly turn the struggling Dodgers into contenders and then champions. He saw Black and he saw a threat. He saw Black and he heard his parents in their bedroom at night whispering about how Blacks were taking over and would be the undoing of America. Then he saw me or he didn't see me. He saw what I represented and he was at once filled with hate.

'An officer was beaten and robbed on base tonight. Nigga looked just like you.'

There was no need to say anymore and especially with the .45 pointing at my head.

I spent the night there on a cold, hard metal bench waiting for Sergeant Cherry to come an identify me. But that was neither the first or the last time I would have a less than a positive encounter with law enforcement. I've since then been slammed to the ground by police and had my teeth shattered.

In other avenues of my life I've shared a fair amount of success having been a middle school teacher, writer and entrepreneur but in law enforcements eyes I am Michael Brown. I am and will be 'just a nigga!

My Man Henry Armstrong

"If it ain't my main man, Henry Armstrong. How you been man? I ain't seen you in a month of Sundays."

"Curtis Jackson," Henry said smiling broadly. "Ain't no accident me bumping into you is it?" Henry said hugging his boyhood friend. Now in their mid fifties the two men had long since parted ways. Henry had taken the more conservative root and had established himself as an integral part of the church and community maintaining his position as a transit worker for the better part of twenty years now.

"What are you doin' now?"

"Was just heading up to Joyce's and say hello before I call it an evening. How've you been Curt and tell me seriously what brings you uptown. You know you don't come uptown unless it's a woman."

"In all honesty I came up here to see you. The phone number I have for you doesn't work so I had to come up here to see you personally."

"I hope you're coming bringing good news."

"It's not bad. Is there somewhere we can grab a beer?"

"Sure let's run over to Small's real quick," Henry said pointing to the bar across the street.

"So whatcha been up to since I last saw you. You still working down on the docks?"

"Yeah. That's all I know. Probably will die there," Curtis said smiling. "Yeah I work days there and then I moonlight standing security at night there."

"Lord knows they didn't put you in charge of security? That's like asking the fox to guard the hen house," Henry laughed.

"Boss man trusts me. I've worked with that man for going on fifteen years now. He thinks Curtis Jackson is the second coming."

"You always could work that charm."

"Just being me brother. Just being me…"

"So what brings you uptown?"

"I told you I came to see my oldest and dearest friend."

"And you said it's not bad news."

"Nah man. I just came to tell you that I'm leaving."

"Leaving?"

"Yeah I saved a few pennies over the years and I just figured it's time for me to get out of this rat race. Figured I'd go down south. You know I got people down in

North Carolina. I'm in the process of buying a nice little piece of land and throwing up a house on it and just kick back. Might even raise some hogs."

"You've been saying that since we were kids. So you're finally gonna do it?"

"I'm leaving in two weeks. Tell me something. When do you retire Henry?"

"I've got another ten or eleven years but they're pushing us towards early retirement with three quarters of our pension. It's not a bad deal but I don't know what I'd do if I didn't work. From their standpoint it's cheaper to bring a new guy in and train him and start him at little or nothing than to keep us around and paying our inflated salaries."

"Gotta admit it makes good business sense but aren't you tired of fighting the crowd every day?"

"Who you asking?"

"So why don't you seriously consider retiring early and come on down to North Carolina with me? New York is alright for young people but after awhile it begins to take its toll."

Henry Armstrong looked at his friend before bursting out in a huge smile.

"You ain't never lied there but I'm like you and the docks. This is all I know."

"But you see I'm giving up both the docks and New York for the chance to improve my quality of life. Who knows? I may add another ten years to this old tired body of mine."

"You're serious?"

"Dead serious and I've got an exit caper that's sure to put a couple of bucks in our pockets for the long haul."

"Oh no. I'm afraid to even ask."

"Don't worry I'm not going to let the cat out of the bag until you decide whether you want to join me or not."

"Wow! You know I haven't seen you in over a year and then you pop up with some life altering propositions and you expect me to drop everything."

"Nah brother. It's not even like that. What I'm offering you is a chance to get out of the madness and go somewhere quieter where you can relax and enjoy the finer things in life. We're not getting any younger you know."

"And let's say I decided to join you what about Joyce?"

"My man Henry Armstrong," Curtis said beer flying from his mouth. "Joyce! How long have you been going with Joyce?"

"Somewhere around sixteen or seventeen years. Why?"

"Because you know as well as I do that Joyce is no more than a convenience. She's like the corner store. The only time you stop by is when you need something. You don't have no intentions of marrying her or anyone else for that matter. All she is is a convenience. And you know as well as I do that there are beautiful women everywhere and with you being a church going man you're gonna have your pick. Besides Joyce is too easy. You need a little more of a challenge at this stage of the game my brother. Change is progress. In any case, think about it I need to know by this time next week. Here take my number."

An hour later, Henry Armstrong sat in the old faded green recliner at Joyce's. It used to be a deep forest green but with the years it had faded to a puke green with worn spots here and there. He was dead tired and he closed his eyes as she went on about something or another. It was Thursday night and they made love on Thursday nights and he only hoped she'd pressed him a shirt so he wouldn't have to go into work looking like

he hadn't been home the night before. And then again if he fell asleep now she may not bother him and just let him sleep.

"Guess who I saw today?"

"Who's that honey?"

"Curtis."

"Get out of here. How's he doing? Is he still working down at the docks?"

"Yeah. You know Curtis is a lifer. Still looks good though."

"You don't see many fifty year olds looking like Curtis. Is he still chiseled and buffed."

"He has been ever since I've known him. He really takes pride and keeps his body in tip-top shape."

"That he does. So what's he talking about?"

"Believe it or not he's talking about retiring and going down south and buying a piece of land and a home."

"Well, he's certainly worked long and hard enough. If anyone deserves that it would be Curtis."

"He asked me to go with him."

"Why don't you? You're another one that's put in their time."

"And what about you?"

"What about me?"

"Would you consider picking up and moving south?"

"I'm forty years old Henry and I grew up a New Yorker. I don't think I can be anything but a New Yorker. I like it here. And it's funny but anywhere I go I compare it and for some reason nothing ever quite compares. I don't know that I could live anywhere else. But I think you should go Henry. I'd come and visit when I could," Joyce said smiling.

They made love for the first time in a long time. When it was over Henry Armstrong lit a cigarette as he dressed.

"Are you seriously considering Curtis' offer?"

"Well, I wasn't until I talked to you but you made me take a second look at it."

"I mean come on Henry. Who are we fooling? We're two lonely people in a city of eight million strangers. When we first met we were curiously in lust. I think over time we've become the best of friends and grown to depend on each other. I love you Henry but I wouldn't be a true friend if I kept you here for selfish reasons. But I think a move south would be good for you. It's time you had the opportunity to kick back on the front porch with a good bottle an just chew and spit the way old men do," Joyce laughed trying to mask the thought of losing her best friend and the only lover she'd had for the last twenty years.

"I resent the old man reference but I have to say you're a good woman, Joyce," Henry said kissing Joyce on the forehead before leaving. He thought of catching the train to go the twelve blocks but the nigh air was warm and he felt like walking.

Curtis and he had been friends ever since he could remember. They were as close as brothers and loved each other dearly.

As kids they were as thick as thieves and most of the boys knew that if they fought one they would inevitably have to fight the other. They'd even gone in the service together under the buddy plan. Henry could still hear his mother's words. 'I know you two love each other but in the end you're going to be the death of each other'. And there were nights when they were still in their early twenties and pulling capers when their number came up and they'd gotten caught and were sent to Rikers for three months. But through it all they had always remained the closest of pals. And neither had seen fit to marry or have kids and now in their mid-fifties retirement seemed like the next logical step. And since Joyce seemed to be alright with it what did he have to hold him. He worked because he knew nothing else and that's just what common folks did. Henry

Armstrong had no excesses aside from a good meal every now and then. And he was not opposed to taking Joyce to Hong Fat down in China Town or for some veal ptarmigan down in Little Italy. But he was tired. New York had overcome him like a heavy fog right before sunup. Curtis had the right idea in mind. Get away to a calmer, more peaceful way of life where he could wile away the hours fishing or listening to smooth jazz with a good bottle and an occasional woman. This was a no-brainer and he was certainly glad Curtis had shown up when he did. There was no telling how long he would have been stuck in the same old rut. He owed New York nothing and in fifty four years he had no ties and nothing him to keep him here in this jungle.

No, he'd call Curtis just as soon as he got home and tomorrow he'd give his two week notice and close out his 401K and tie up any loose ends with the bank. For all intensive purposes he was out.

Cutis was ecstatic when he heard the news.

"Man you've made a good decision. I'm gonna email you pictures of the place and the land. You're gonna love it but I don't want you to jump in and have regrets later so if you're not doing anything this weekend we can fly down and you can see it firsthand."

"Nah man. I trust your judgment. If you say it's on point then I'll take your word for it. You've always had impeccable taste."

"And man this is better—I mean far superior—than any home I've had here in the city. I couldn't afford to buy this home in New York but down there where property is much cheaper it looks like a small estate in comparison to what you'd get for the same money here."

"I hear you. I'm gonna put in my two week notice today. I'm so ready to put New York behind me. I'm glad you showed up when you did."

"Did you get a chance to run it by Joyce?"

"Yeah. I guess you were right about us. She gave me her blessing and told me to go. Said she can always come visit."

"How you feeling about that partner?"

"A little relieved that she took it so well but then it bothers me that she did take it so well. I mean after seventeen years it was a little disheartening for her to dismiss my leaving so lightly. You know what I'm saying? I mean after seventeen years to just say 'Go. You have my blessings'."

Curtis laughed.

"A woman's a funny thing. You know the older I get the more I realize how little I know about them."

"You said you had something planned before we left."

"Just a little caper…. Nothing serious or dangerous… Just a little caper to line our pocket with some spending change when we get to North Carolina… I've been working on it for more than a year. But I'll tell you more about it later on. It'll be the last thing we do right before we leave."

"You know there's a lotta brothers upstate who are doing twenty-five to life who said the same thing. You know, 'it s just a little caper nothing serious or dangerous'."

Curtis laughed.

"My man Henry Armstrong. That's why I love you man. Always the skeptic… But let me ask you this. Have I ever been upstate? But you're right. Guess you're just going to have to trust me on this one."

Henry Armstrong was apprehensive but Curtis was right. He'd been running small capers since he was in high school and had never been charged or convicted of anything. And the one time they'd spent any time in the pokey was not because of anything they'd done or overlooked but because of a woman Curtis was double-dipping on. She'd been eaves dropping trying to get wind of Curtis' cheating on her and learned of the heist. Soon after she confirmed Curtis' cheating and dropped a dime on them.

They'd gotten off on a technicality but that was the last time he'd had a brush with the law.

Still, Henry was so caught up in the fact that he was finally making his exodus the caper or whatever Curtis had planned seemed trivial in comparison. Standing at the toll booth at the entrance to the Holland Tunnel Henry Armstrong said his customary 'Have a blessed day' he smiled. He hated the job. He always had but he'd persevered in spite of it. It paid the bills and that had been enough. Now he had a chance for more. No longer did he simply have to be content to exist nameless, faceless in this mindless, madness. Curtis had given him the opportunity to dream, to dream of living again. He had never really considered anything other than that moment. He moved because he was supposed to. He went to work because he was supposed to. He went to church on Sundays because he was supposed to. He was if nothing else a strong man, a pillar of the community because he had to be. But not once had he considered his life and given any thought to what it was that he wanted to do. Up 'til now he just did what he was supposed to do.

Grabbing a six pack on his way home he considered stopping by Joyce's and then thought better of it. He didn't know what it was he was feeling as far as she was concerned. She seemed almost contrite when she told him to go. But she did tell him what he refused to see for far too long. They were there out of need not want and used each other to fulfill their own personal needs. They were civil with nary a mean word uttered to the other over the years because there was no passion. In all the years there had never been any love. Just need and she had let him know in no uncertain terms that she recognized it as a charade but she had overlooked it as long as he fulfilled her needs.

He was if nothing else her constant. It was all a little cold but it was what it was. No. There was no need to stop by Joyce's. He was tired of her and the cold, monotonous sex that had become so routine.

Henry Armstrong was a new man. He was a man with hope and a dream of Southern churches and barbeques and fishing. He dreamed of sitting out a cold beer in one hand watching the baseball game. He dreamed of that beautiful black stallion that

was as bright as she was pretty. Yes, this is what Henry Armstrong dreamed. This is the life that he'd always dreamed of and now would have.

In the next week, the days seemed to crawl by. He still hadn't heard from Curtis but he knew Curtis and knew that if nothing else he prided himself on being dependable. As soon as he got the call from Curtis he'd planned on calling in sick and use up some of his sick days but for now work kept him busy and his mind off his dream. Fit to be tied Henry threw his black leather on and headed out the door. Twenty minutes later he was at Small's. Two doubles later he found himself at Joyce's door.

"Well, hello stranger," she said smiling and pulling her robe closed. "I wasn't sure if you'd left o not."

"You know I wouldn't leave without coming to see my baby."

"I wasn't so sure after what I told you the last time. We both know what I said was true. I may have been a little to candid in my honesty but we're not children."

"I think I knew it. It wasn't the presentation. It was the delivery. Why didn't you just cut my heart out?"

"If I had sugar-coated it you would have felt guilty for leaving me and may have even stayed so as not to hurt me. I know you Henry Armstrong. You're a good strong principled man. You will hurt yourself rather than hurt someone else but if I love you and I do I'm not going to stand in your way and let you defer your own happiness on account of me. That would be selfish and my love for you won't let me stand in your way.

"I love you Joyce," Henry said grabbing the petite nurse in front of him.

"I know you do Henry. I've never doubted that for a minute. My problem was that you were never *in love* with me. Maybe you'll find someone and fall in love in North Carolina. I'm already green-eyed with envy. I can't even imagine you really being in love. You're not built like that but I'll tell you what when you do that's gonna be one lucky woman cause you have never been in love with me and I have never had a man treat me any better than you have Henry Armstrong. She'll be one lucky woman that's for damn sure."

Henry lost track of how many times they made love that night. He felt better knowing that he'd been a good man to this woman even though he never had committed to her or any woman. Joyce was right. It just wasn't in him.

Two more days and no call. He wondered if Curtis was alright. Had his little caper backfired? And then as if he knew Henry was waiting by the phone Cutis called.

"You ready to go?"

"Just been waiting for your call."

"You packed?"

"A few toiletries. Joyce is going to ship the rest."

"Okay. We go tomorrow night. Can you meet me downtown? Say Nathan's Times Square at twelve."

"I'll see you there."

Later that afternoon Henry stood at a table in Nathan's. He couldn't remember how many times they'd met here over the years. Dressed in a jean shirt, jeans and a pair of penny loafers Henry always had to smile when he saw Curtis who was always

fastidious when it came to the clothes that he put on his well manicured body.

"Looking smooth as usual," Henry said hugging his oldest and dearest friend.

"I try," he said smiling grateful for the compliment and handing Henry and

envelope. "I just spoke to my lawyer and the real estate broker. The key to the house is

in the envelope as well as the address so Joyce can mail your belongings."

I took the envelope and put it in my inside pocket.

"So, we're really going to do this."

"Yes sir. Now let me run this caper by you," Curtis said.

An hour later I was back on the A train headed uptown. Curtis had made the

whole thing seem like just another walk in the park but I had my druthers. Unlike Curtis

I was always fearful. To me a little fear was a good thing. We used to argue but there

was no argument. A firm believer in Murphy's Law I knew that what can go wrong will

go wrong. I was not only skeptical but pessimistic despite Curtis downplaying it as a

piece of cake.

Still, I had to trust and have faith in his judgment. He'd never led me wrong

before and I would never have been able to think about relocating if I hadn't had a few

dollars in the bank from our other capers.

When I arrived home I took a hot shower and laid down with the intentions of

taking a nap knowing full well that I wouldn't be able to sleep as loud as my heart was

pounding. All I knew was that my love hate relationship with New York was over. It had come time for us to part ways and I guess any change as drastic as this just naturally came with some anxiety. And then there was the damn caper which never seemed as easy as Curtis would have you believe. Hell, I'd spent my whole life saving the few pennies I could and now that I was fashioned to sit back and enjoy it Curtis was risking

us both. I knew if I was well off enough to retire Curtis had to be as well. This wasn't necessary and could mess up everything. For a long time now I knew that Curtis was financially stable but it was like wok for him. He had to earn. Money gave him his sense of worth. The capers on the other hand gave him his buzz, his rush, his thrill. I don't know if it was the excitement of living on the edge or the same excitement that a junkie feels when he takes that first hit. Henry just hoped he stayed true to his word about this being the last one.

Henry slept until early evening. When he awoke it was already past six. Scrambling to get himself together he took a hot shower and dressed quickly before throwing his razor and toothbrush in his overnight bag and hurried out the door. He wanted to stop by and say goodbye to Joyce but thought better of it. That could get sticky and he hated long goodbyes. Besides he only had a little more than an hour to be down at the docks and be in position. Jumping on the A train Henry headed back downtown. He was supposed to be there at seven and he was cutting it close. It was already six fifteen and he still had a ways to go. At six thirty he walked the final block to the docks.

When he arrived he was surprised to see the flashing lights. There were police cars and ambulances everywhere. Making his way through the crowd he moved as close to the yellow tape as was possible. There were police everywhere.

"What happened officer?" Henry asked a female officer pacing back and forth trying to keep the unruly crowd from crossing the yellow tape.

"Looks to be a robbery that went sour," she responded barely acknowledging him.

"Was anybody hurt?"

"The night watchman was shot and one of the thieves. Why are you asking sir? Do you have anything to do with this?"

"No ma'am. I'm just here to pick up my friend. We had plans to go out tonight." I said now careful to avoid any connection with the whole foiled fiasco.

"And who is your friend?"

"He works as the night security guard," I said.

"You may want to check with EMS," she said pointing to one of the ambulances blocking the street and loading a body on a stretcher.

I rushed over fearful of what I was about to encounter only to see Curtis lying on a stretcher while two EMS workers worked feverishly to hook up an IV. It was obvious that he was in excruciating pain. When he saw me smiled that big ol' smile I'd come to know so well.

"My man Henry Armstrong," he said garnering all the strength he could muster to get the words out.

"What happened Curtis?"

"I brought in the James boys to spare you the drama. Didn't think it fair that I got you involved. Now I wish I had."

"So, what happened?"

Curtis summoned me to lean over so the EMS workers couldn't hear. The blood was flowing from the gunshot wounds somewhere in his stomach or chest. It was hard to tell with his uniform still on.

"Excuse me sir. I'm going to give you a shot to alleviate some of the pain. It's a little morphine. They'll give you something a little stronger when we get to St. Luke's but this will have to do for now."

I moved aside to let the worker administer the shot then leaned down to hear what my friend had to say.

"Like I said I brought in the James boys—you know 'em—to spare you the headache and everything went according to plan. Then when we were planning to leave and on the way out the door the younger one Justin turned around and shot me and took the bags I was carrying. Known them all my life. I never thought they would do this to me."

"I'll take care of them," I said. I'd never trusted them and didn't particularly care for either of them. They were Curtis' friends.

"No. You have the keys to the house in Carolina. Take Joyce and go and get it ready. I'll be along directly," Curtis said wincing in pain.

"Are you riding with your friend sir?" the EMS worker asked.

"No, I'll meet you at the hospital. You're taking him to St. Lukes if I'm correct?"

"Yes sir. That's where he requested we take him."

"Okay. I'll meet you there," I said as I climbed out of the ambulance before glancing over at my friend who was now unconscious.

"I don't believe that'll be necessary sir," the EMS worker said. "I'm listing the time of death at six fifty eight," she said closing his eyes.

Purple and Grape

"All I find I keep," was all the tall Black man hooded man said sticking the gun in my side.

"Brother, I just finished putting in eight hours for the man six days outta the last seven days. You have to be outta your fuckin' mind if you believe I'm going to give you shit," I was never more serious. This nigga would have to kill me first.

"Niggas dying out here everyday. I don't give a fuck. Now give up the cash."

I turned to face him. He didn't seem to be a bad brother just a brother like a whole lotta brothers that had fallen on bad times.

"C'mon brother let me buy you a shot and we'll talk about it."

"Nigga is you kiddin' me. I can buy myself my own shot when you empty your pockets," he said the boldness leaving his voice.

"I ain't givin' you shit and if you shoot me you're not only gonna have me on your conscience but the cops on your ass and for what a couple of hundred dollars? Then you gonna be runnin' for the rest of your life. And like I said for what—a couple of hundred dollars—be for real. Come on let's go grab a couple of beers."

Somehow I must've gotten through and minutes later we were making our way down 8th Avenue towards Small's.

All the usual folks were there for happy hour.

"What up Stretch?"

"I'm good?"

"How you doing Blue? You certainly looking like everything is going your way."

"I try," she said knowing she was looking just as good as she wanted to. I'd always meant to follow up with her and to this day don't know why I hadn't. "Who's your friend?"

I hadn't had a chance to get my boys name. It wasn't as if we'd met at a meet and greet over wine.

"Go ahead man. Introduce yourself while I head to the little boy's room," I said taking my leave.

When I returned the two were engrossed in what seemed a rather lively conversation.

"I like your friend Sharif. He has some interesting ideas on a number of issues," Blue said smiling.

Yeah. His issues had me wanting to beat him down on the one hand and thanking God I wasn't in his shoes on the other.

"You said Sharif has some interesting views. Care to expound? I'd like to hear his views on Black-on-Black crime in the ghetto," I said eyeing him closely.

"Oh, that's just so trite, so mundane. His ideas—at least the ones he's shared with me—are so fresh and provocative. Why would you want to speak of something so trite? What intelligent Black man even thinks there is a need for conversation when it comes to that?"

"Nonetheless I'd like to hear Mr. Sharif's views," I said my eyes never leaving the brother's face. I think you'd find Mr. Sharif's views on Black-on-Black crime may surprise you."

"What you asking me brother? You asking me if I would stick up another Black man to feed my daughter? If that's the question you're asking me then you already know. Would I commit a crime for that same little Black girl. Hell yeah."

I smiled looking over at Blue who was shaken by his words.

"You're adamant in your ignorance, Sharif," I said ordering another round.

"Adamant only in your world. My world's a whole lot different baby and the only thing that's ignorant is that you have taken on a culture in which you see yourself as being bout it bout it and have bought into a system that defiles, denigrates, degrades, debases, disparages you then when you serve no other purpose it dismisses you and sends you to and makes you a ward of the Department of Corrections. That's my world.

You play chess man? If you did you'd see that they—the powers that be—have you in check. But then again you probably wouldn't even recognize that you're no more than a pawn in the whole scheme of things in the game of life my brother. You have not come to recognize that though have you?" Sharif laughed. "You can't because although your body's free your mind is still in shackles. Look at you in your Jos A Banks suit."

"Armani," I corrected.

"Exactly what I'm talking about. Look at you quoting the name of someone you've never met. Yet, you're running around like you're a moving billboard wearing his name on your back. Brother you're exactly the Negro Malcolm was talking about when he said…

"Oh, and I say it again, you've been had. You've been took. You've been hoodwinked. Bamboozled. Led astray. Run amok!"

He's talking about you my brother," Sharif concluded. You have no knowledge of self. You have bought into his identity. You have let him brainwash you into what it is that he wants you to be. He has defined you my brother."

"What do you mean Sharif? You're losing me. Stretch has not been brainwashed. If anything he's one of the clearest thinks I know. I don't know how long you've known him but you're not going to find a better bother. He's decent. He ain't tryna be down with nothin' or nobody. He's a rare find nowadays. He's one of the few brothers that defines himself and the road he travels. And to top that he does it with a bit of flair and he's a gentleman. You don't find that nowadays. Tell me something Sharif? How long have you known Stretch?"

Sharif smiled.

"I have to admit that I just met the brother."

"And he's buying you drinks and you're hatin' on him like that? Is there something I missed?"

"Yeah. There's quite a bit you missed Blue but let's put that on hold for the moment. The fact of the matter is your man Shariff uses the term brother so freely and loosely that I half-way want to believe we are but anytime you treat your brother with less than the dignity he deserves you can't be considered a brother of mine."

"When I use the term brother I am only endearing myself to you so we can sit and converse. It does not mean I accept you into my clan. If you speak English and live in America and I speak Spanish and live in Spain we would have a hard time communicating. Therefore we could not be brothers culturally because we do not speak the same language and have little shared experience. I am sorry to say but we live in two different worlds. It is no different here in Harlem. I have white neighbors who live next door that do not speak to me because they do not what to say. They know that their interests are not mine and I know that mine are not theirs. And that's okay and I accept that but what bothers me more is that there are too many brothers like you Stretch. There are too many brothers that move up to Harlem because nowadays it's the trendy thing to do. We do share the same experiences but instead of acknowledging the experiences we shared as a people you and your kind try to act as if it never existed. Are you ashamed of who you are and where you come from?"

"Aren't you making a lot of accusations considering you don't know this man? Did you know that he attended Howard University, an historically Black university?"

Shariff laughed again.

"Whoa! Slow down sister. Stretch is a big boy. He can defend himself. Why are you being so overprotective anyway?"

"Cause its happy hour. And we come here damn near every night to laugh, and talk and unwind and put the day behind us. We don't come here to criticize and hate on each other."

"It's no more than two supposedly strong Black men from different sides of the track sharing our experiences. No harm in that is there?"

"You're the only one talking. I don't get the sharing part."

"I'm sure when I finish my little soliloquy Stretch will say his part," Sharif said smiling at Blue before finishing off the glass.

"Let him finish Blue. I'm curious as to where he's going with this."

"We walk the same streets everyday and we are as far apart as the moon and the sky and do you know why?"

"Please continue," Stretch said.

"Well there are many reasons but the primary reason is because what Carter G. Woodson so aptly named his book. It is because of the miseducation of the Negro. The first thing he did was to place himself in our lives as master. When he assumed this position he made us understand very quickly that we were no longer required to think. Instead he would do the thinking for us. And so for the first two hundred years in this country all choices and decisions were made for us by the master. Reading would increase thought and make a Negro say 'what if' so books were forgiven. And being that we were unable to think and because it was easier not to think we listened and we did what the master said even if what is we were doing for us was detrimental to our very lives.

Nothing's changed except that he has perfected the miseducation of the Negro to the extent that we are lost in the need for upward mobility with no clear end plan in sight."

"Oh my God. Are you telling me the quest for upward mobility is a bad thing?"

"By no means Blue. Upward mobility is a beautiful thing taken in the right context. Don't get me wrong."

"And what is the right context?" Blue asked.

"That's a good question and one that so many of us got wrong following the Civil Rights Movement. There's a good reason why we are in such a precarious situation today. We took Dr. King's message of respect and equality to mean material equality and in our haste to be seen as Americans equal in all respect we lost sight of everything. We who

had been the purveyors of knowledge within our segregated communities now saw the

edifice of tall buildings as improvement. But it was the indoctrination of our minds that

so bothered me. We fought saying the pledge of allegiance because we did not consider

ourselves a part of this non-United States of America but we did not recognize all the

other ways in which we were hoodwinked and bamboozled. We bought into the idea that

upward mobility simply meant amassing wealth and material items. At the same time a

people without roots and without a culture can be shaped, molded and shaped. There is

no reference point to look back on for clarification. There is no governing body, no

guidance, no law of the land. There is no Moses on the mountain with the tablet

containing the Ten Commandments.

Oh, there was Dr. King and Malcolm and a host of others our young people will

never come to know because they have been dissuaded from searching for the truth or

coming to know themselves and whence they come. And as you and I both know if you

cut off the head you kill he body. This wasn't by accident. And once there was no one to

guide you. It became leadership by proxy and came in so many forms. But one of the

most devastating ways it was employed was by the media. Your utilitarianism suddenly

became a priority. You may not have been able to serve in the First World War but you

can serve the needs of this country now in so many ways. And since they have taken over the ways in which they not teach but indoctrinate us into being malleable misfits and miscreants we are still shackled. They have taken our will to think and somehow indoctrinated us to simply react instead making us some kin to Piaget's dogs that simply replied to stimuli. That is who we have become. This is our evolution.

Now our children who are in such dire need of love and guidance and education have been turned over, relinquished to the very same man who enslaved our bodies so that he can now enslave our mind while we go in search of another dollar.

Black parents have left their children in the midst of the enemy that has raped and lynched them since for generations and asked them to educate them. Our children! Our most precious resources! Why niggas you have lost your minds. So, nowadays if you ask a thirteen year old who Nat Turner or even Joe Biden is they have no idea. But they can tell you what the number thirteen looks like when it comes to a pair of Nike Jordans.

And you're no better walking around mindless talkin' about in your Armani suit. What are you doing?"

"What do mean what am I doing?"

"Our parents taught me as well as anyone within earshot that we had a responsibility to ourselves as well as every other Black person that once we got up out of the muck and mire to pull the ext Negro out but we can only lead if we know whence we come from and who we followed. We have always followed men of great being, great intellect, and wisdom and they have led us from despair to hope of a new day. And never has that man been compromised or been able to be bought out by a shiny suit and a fancy car. But now our sights have been shifted and our focus changed. And in the process we've lost our identity, our moral turpitude and have been assimilated, acculturating his mongrel culture whose god is capitalism and who will do anything for it. That is who I see when I see you in your Armani suit and Italian loafers.

Upward mobility does not mean we simply imitate white folks buying patterns. Upward mobility doesn't mean neglecting our children to purchase a Benz or Audi or that home with the two car garage and abandon our children to make time and a half. Upward mobility does not mean turning our children over to their network programming which tells them that they need this and that at fifteen minute intervals yet not giving them the smarts or the critical thinking skills to differentiate between what they need and what Madison Avenue insists they must have to keep up with the rest of the boys and girls in America.

Have you ever taken a look at our children today?"

"I'll agree they are nothing to be proud of," Blue admitted.

"No. I mean have you ever looked at our kids on a purely superficial level?"

"I'm not sure I know what you mean."

"I'm talking about the way they dress, the way they talk. Here you are in money making Manhattan the center of capitalism for the world. You have Madison Avenue prescribing what we wear, how we dress. Move over to Fashion Avenue wear these clothes are first put on the streets of America. We are the center but isn't it funny that in a matter of weeks these poor urban kids that can't see their way out of the city are imitated across America."

"You do have a point."

"I know I do. Our kids are on the front lines and we are not doing anything about it. We have become so selfish with our own desires that we have forgotten our children. So, instead of us teaching them and securing the real upward mobility, that is the teaching of our children about things that are truly relevant such as our history, and the way in which we treat ourselves and our fellow man we leave them instead to the networks and their depictions of us which we now use to define us. It's truly heart rendering and yet we are so busy seeking acceptance and waiting to say we made it that we've forgotten what it is that is important to us."

"And what is it that's important to us since you're the spokesperson for all Black people?"

"Listen, I don't pretend to be a spokesperson for all Black people. All I try to do is be educated, aware and conscious of how I live my life and what it means to be a strong, intelligent, Black man in today's world. If I can do that then I can at least present a positive Black role model to today's America. I can only do what I can do in my current position but I can be the best of in whatever role He gives me.

But I am aware which is why I don't champion goods from the country that still has the majority of us locked up in mental slavery.

Here. Let me give you an example of what I'm talking about. Back in the day when Nike first came out they were like any other startup company struggling to get along. At the same time Michael Jordan was a young player just starting to make a name for himself when Philip Knight the founder of Nike decided to give Mike a call. The rest is history.

Michael went on to become the greatest player to ever play the game. Nike rode Michael's coattails and went on to become one of the biggest companies in the world.

Mike got a stipend in relation to what Nike made because his face was the forefront for the company. Now kids who have no education, no marketable skills and can't scrape two nickels together to make a dime suddenly feel compelled to run out and buy a pair of two hundred dollar sneakers. If their mommy's and daddy's don't buy them they feel no remorse for robbing or stealing them.

They've been so inundated and programmed by capitalism. I bought some New Era caps awhile back to resale and was riding with a friend of mine's son one day. When he opened the box the kid lost his mind. Started telling me that they were 'official snapbacks'. I asked him what makes them official. He couldn't tell me that or what separated them from the old snapback that my daddy used to wear to cut the grass. He couldn't tell me but he wanted to buy the same cap that my father used to pay a dollar for. Only now it had a company logo on it which made it 'official' and sold for forty dollars.

He was typical. He had the beginnings of dreadlocks which was all the latest fad and a Bob Marley t-shirt on. Now I grew up with Bob Marley and considered him—as many did—a prophet and so with the combination of hair do and shirt on I was curious as to why he donned both. He, however, didn't have a clue as to who the man was he wore on the front of his shirt or what his dreads represented. He knew nothing more than it was the latest style donned by other teens his age. In other words it was the latest fashion. Funny thing though, his mother who graduated Magna Cum Laude from a most prestigious university in the northeast would sit down at night and twist his hair for him and at other times would send him to her beauty parlor at other times to have his hair done had never questioned either his choice of hair dos or his wearing of the Marley shirt. She had never considered asking him why he made the choices he did. In other words, he received no other information than what the media and his peers had given him and so he wore the hair do and shirt with no other information other than that it was popular."

"Shariff, why are you telling us all this? I mean really. I get all that. But why are you telling us all this? It's no different with white kids who wear swastikas and Confederate flags and shoot nine innocent churchgoers in Charlestown, South Carolina. I just heard an interview by jazz trumpeter Branford Marsalis where he said that teenagers don't act they react. In other words teenagers don't think they simply react to the stimuli presented them." Blue said.

"My point exactly. And I have no problem with that. My problem is that we are not white folks. And we as Black folks have an obligation not only to ourselves but to our children to be equipped with the knowledge and baton to pick up the struggle ad lead us into the next generation. We all come into this world as a blank slate. It is up to us as Black folks, as parents to do what our parents did for us. We do not need another Michael Brown, Freddie Gray or Eric Garner to wake us from our malaise. It is not at these times that we should be shocked but if we know the history of our people in this country then there is no way we should be shocked. We do not have the luxury of looking at President Obama and acknowledge that we have somehow made it as a people. No. We should see Obama for what he is. An anomaly… But he is in no way representative of all Black folks in America; the majority of whom remain poor and uneducated. We can be extremely proud that he has risen to the heights that he has. It is instead, our job, our responsibility to pick up Dr. King's mantle and repair the disconnect that has purposely been put in place to sow the chords of discontent. No longer is it sufficient to simply rest on the laurels of our president and say that since he's in the White House that we have made it as a people. This is simply not true. I'm not sure if it's social media or just the media in general but I can't remember seeing this many Black men being killed by cops in my lifetime as I've seen under his watch. The fact is we have not arrived. But Black folks are easily pacified and are under the impression that we have finally arrived."

"And so you are angry at the world and you believe that because you feel this way that we have as a people lost focus?"

"I do."

"And what may I ask makes you different than me," I asked.

"It depends on whose eyes and perception I am viewed from. From a bigoted white cops point of view there is little or difference between you and I. But does it matter how he perceives me? Not in the least. I cannot try to work on him and work on me as well. Life is too short. But what I can do is resolve to stay both educated, informed so that I can avoid all confrontations with him and know how to diffuse a situation which favors him and not because of his superior intellect but simply because he has a gun and no regard for my life. I just believe it is our job to teach and address our children around the systemic pitfalls designed towards the genocide of Black men. I simply believe that if equip our young men with their history in this great country of ours and all that we have had to overcome and continue to teach and educate them and try to help them to understand we could lessen so many of the obstacles put in place to maim and limit their overall growth. Education is the key and I'm not speaking of formal education per se. I am speaking of the education of a man such as yourself that has in some ways mastered this America dilemma that looks to eradicate us all which we know as racism.

This is our responsibility. We are supposed to educate our young men who are not aware that the drug trade so glamorized by Pacino in Scarface is not an avenue out of poverty but a means of keeping you in. You must teach him that this is film and not reality. In reality, the drug trade is a means of putting you in the system and keeping the unemployment statistics down. With drugs comes guns, more crime and the elimination of stable family units. That's only from our perspective.

However, from their perspective it keeps unemployment down. Just think of how many jobs are secured every time a young Black man is arrested for intent to sell and distribute.

There are the police, social services, emergency care, hospitals, social services, the judicial system and the prison system. We're in the drug trade with this Horatio Algers dream of going from rags to riches in a day and that just doesn't happen that way but again the media started with this introduction as an avenue to a life of glamour and wealth in the late seventies and he early eighties with the dawn of Superfly and Scarface.

And with no guidance and unable to think we actually looked at it as a viable way to eradicate poverty and other ills that plagued us."

"Okay. I've heard enough my brother. And I must agree with you whole heartedly. But I don't think you can arbitrarily pick people and make allegations because they don't dress like you.

I don't dress like you because there was a strong Black man in my life and he taught me everything you say that our young men need to be taught. I remember back in the sixties when the Panthers and other groups wore afros and dashikis. They were my heroes and I had the utmost respect for them but I wasn't going to don the clothing that white folks saw as the apparel of the defiant and rebellious. I understood but I could neither feed my son or educate him if I were in a five by eight cell so I wore that which was less confrontational only to stay one step ahead of the powers that be. If you know which group he's targeting I think it smart that you take the bulls eye off your back.

Still, I see no difference between you and me my brother so why target me? Know your enemy and know that I am not him. His aim is to divide and conquer. Our differences my brother is at subtle as the difference between purple and grape."

Tommy and Jalil

"How many years we been covering this route Jalil?"

"I don't know. I think I've been doing it for about nine years. Together I believe it's close to seven."

"That's right. And in those seven years I think the ol' man Henry's only given me two fifty cents cost of living raises," the young white boy commented exasperated.

"I guess the cost of living doesn't go up in my neighborhood."

"What are you saying man? Are you trying to tell me that you've never received a raise in nine years?"

"Not a dime."

"Are you serious?"

"Have you ever known me to lie to you?" the older man said.

"No. And you mean to tell me you never approached the old man and said anything or asked for one?"

"Oh, I started once but he grew all defensive like and got angry saying something like 'are you telling me that you're not happy with what I'm paying you? You know a lot of your people would be happy with just having a job and you're complaining' so I just let it go. I had to think about my girls."

"Ah, man that ain't right. You want me to go and speak to him?"

"Then we'll both be on the unemployment line. Don't get it twisted. Don't think that just because you're white he has any more respect for you than he has for us. To him poor white trash is the same as being a nigga."

"I ain't no po' white trash."

"Didn't mean nothin' by it Tommy but that's the way he looks at you. Face it. We got no skills and he knows it. He can drive by the Urban Ministry and pick up three or four men off the street and replace us in half a heartbeat."

"Then why doesn't he do that? The cheap bastard…" Tommy said jumping from the truck and grabbing the old worn out mattress and throwing it onto the back of the garbage truck before climbing on the side of the truck and sticking his head in the window. "Man most of the trucks have two men riding to do the heavy lifting. Here it's just me and this shit is getting old fast."

"I hear you. But don't get it twisted the only reason he keeps us on is that he trusts us. He knows when he sends us out we get the job done and there's never a complaint. We're hard-working and dependable. But that don't mean he won't fire your ass if there's a problem."

"Yeah so what he does is take us for granted. He acts like we don't even exist. Shit I'm trying to eat too. You know what I'm saying? If me and ma had to live off of what he pays me we'd starve to death. Plus I'm thirsty. I want more."

"I understand," the older man said smiling. "I was once young too you know. But if you're really thirsty what you can do is go back to school and make something out of your life. You're young and don't have the responsibility of raising a family. You live at home with your mom and I know she'd be happy just knowing you were trying to better yourself."

"You're right but what he's doing still ain't right."

"Son, I learned a long time ago that right ain't nothing but a direction you turn. It ain't nothing more than that. And more people been killed in the name of right than any other reason. You just don't know son. More people have been wronged in the name of right than you can shake a stick at. Now are you sure you want to take a stand in the name of right?"

"I hear what you're saying Jalil but I just can't stand by and let him treat us like this."

"That's youth talking. You're young. That's all it is. I'm old but trust me though you don't get old being no fool. What I suggest you do is keep working and bide your time. Maybe take a couple of classes at night and plan on getting out of here, and make a better life for yourself."

"I got you. And I think I will go back to school. You know I used to do alright in school. Made honor roll a couple of times and you know I do alright without this sellin' a little weed. I mean I ain't really getting' paid but it keeps me in paper. To tell you the truth I really don't need this garbage shit except that I got in a little trouble a few years back and got ten years probation."

"Trust me there ain't no future in selling drugs. The more you sell, the more money you bring in the higher your chances are of getting caught. My younger brother thought the same thing and he's doing five to ten now."

"I hear you Ja. I don't plan on it being no career or nothing. I'm just doing it 'til I can figure out what my next move is. You feel me?"

"I do and I don't know if I should tell you this or not but believe me I'm not trying to glorify it but I used to hustle a lil bit myself."

"Get outta here," Tommy said the grin illuminating his face.

"Have you ever heard of Casper?"

"Yeah they said that nigga ran everything from 112th Street on up to the Bronx. Did you know him?"

Jalil smiled.

"Yeah I knew him. Everybody knew him right 'til he went upstate to do a bid," the old man said pausing before he continued. "I did five years on some petty, trumped up charges and never, not once did any of my running partners come to see me. Not one.

But I used those five years. It gave me time to think and when it was all over I came to realize a lot of things. One of the things I learned is that the streets don't love nobody. I lost everything that I had materially and when it came time to pay to the piper the only people that were around were those that warned me about the streets from jump. And that was family.

Those were some of the roughest days of my life. I learned a lot during that time though. I learned that friends come and go. But in the end family will always be there for you. I didn't hear or maybe I just didn't want to hear them in the beginning so caught up was I in the game but in the end that's all I heard were their words. And you know why I finally heard them?"

"Why's that Ja-?"

"Because in the end it wasn't those gun totin' brothers by my side it was my family who had my back. I was like the prodigal son and they were simply waiting in the wings for me to come on home. You understand me son?"

"I think I do. But on the real—tell me seriously—were you really Casper?"

"I guess I was at one time. At least that's what they tell me."

"Man you was a legend."

"I was a fool is what I was. I missed my girls growing up. And for what? For a few dollars?"

"A few dollars. Man back in the day you had to be worth millions," Tommy said still grinning broadly.

The old man chuckled to himself.

"That's what they say. But you know where I live?"

"Yeah. Queens Village or Hollis."

"That's right. I've lived in the same house I've lived in for twenty seven years. I raised both my girls there and been driving the same car for the last sixteen years. That's how I got the name Caspar. I was like a ghost and I prided myself for keeping it low key and under the radar. Now I had some fellas who I ran with at the time that are still upstate because they had to let the world know they was high rollers but I ain't never had no affinity for mens or being locked up like a caged animal so I kept it low key but if they even get a hint or a whisper that you're rising above your station in life believe me they're coming after ya."

"So what did you do with all that money?"

"I invested wisely," Jalil said smiling his toothy grin.

"Oh my God. So, why do you take this shit and drive this ol' fucked up garbage truck and take that shit from the old man?"

"Because like you I have a probation officer that needs to know that I am gainfully employed. And I believe that it is smart to always keep a low profile and stay under the radar. Besides there is nothing wrong with putting in a hard day's work to keep a sense of one's worth. And as far as the old man goes, he will have to own his life and actions in the end. He can't do anything to me. He can only hurt himself when it comes Judgment Day and he has to meet His maker. Then he will have to atone for how he lived his life and treated his fellow man. I know this may not make sense to you at your age. How old are you now Tommy?"

"Twenty six. I'll be twenty-seven at the beginning of next month."

"I think I was about the same age when I first got started out. And I started the same way too selling a little weed. By the time I was thirty five most of the weed and other drugs that hit Harlem came through me. Now with two little girls of my own at home all I can do is ask God the Father for forgiveness for all the hell I brought to other people's lives but I don't expect for you to hear me at your age."

"I hear you man and that's why I only sell weed. I ain't trying to have that on my conscious no matter how much money I can make."

"Then maybe you are further along than I was. I mean more mature. It wasn't even for the money. For me it was just something that I was good at so I did it. Now I'm doing my penance but if I can offer you any advice so that it may help make life a little easier I would tell you to keep your life simple and avoid the pitfalls aimed at poor people like you and me. They're put there purposely and it's a bit like quicksand. The more you wriggle the deeper you sink. So, you have to begin to think of life on the more spiritual side and no matter what you do there is a certain finality to any life that you lead. And that's death so you have to reconsider your true worth.

What do you want to be remembered for? You begin to think of your legacy and not only how you want to be remembered but what you did to be remembered for. I want to be remembered for being there and being able to help in some shape or fashion. I want to be remembered for having something to offer that in turn made the next man better but I never want to be remembered for the superficial. He looked good. He had money. No, in essence it is who you are and how close a similarity did you run to his life that is the true measure of who you are?"

"I hear you."

"The material things that often tend to drive us pale in comparison to what life is really about and if you try to live in a certain way. If you follow in His way life becomes simple yet full if you understand what I'm saying. But first you have to change your mindset and find the true essence and ask yourself the tough questions.

Why is it so important that you chase the dollar and what did you really get once you had it. Did you fulfill your need?

Ask yourselves those questions. Accept Him to give you what is that you need to fulfill the void in you. The search for the dollar will never fulfill that void. Only he can. Ask Him to and come to know the goodness of life. Do not stop or slow down long enough to ask and you will forever be blind to peace and happiness Tommy."

"That's some deep shit Jalil but you know I can honestly say that I feel where you're coming from. You know I've had a couple of nice rides and at the time I thought that was what was important to me. But the novelty wore off two weeks later when those car payments came but on the real money doesn't get it done for me. It's like there's gotta be something other than let me get this paper so I can run out and get some shit I don't need. And when you get home that night I still have to smoke that blunt 'cause you're still fiendin'. So, I feel you on the whole unfulfilled thang you was talkin' but I don't know if I'm ready to try that whole religion thang quite yet," Tommy laughed.

"You sound like you're afraid?"

"Why you say that?"

"Because I was the same way. You see I didn't know of another way of life but the one I was living and as bad as it was it was all that I knew and I have to admit that although it wasn't much when it came to substance it was still the only thing I knew. So, when a brother approached me I was the same way you are like oh shit he's tryin' to change my entire life, the whole way I do things. But you know he did it the way it should be done. He told me his experience once and I never heard mention of it again. I was the one that went in search of it to help me understand the world I lived in and my place in it. And it's funny but I found Him under my terms and He embraced me. And no longer is there that void and many of my questions have been answered and my dilemmas put the rest. End of story."

"I'm gonna give that a lot of thought tonight. I definitely think it's time for a change," Tommy said jumping from the truck and heading for his car. "Talk to you tomorrow Ja- and tell the girls I said hi for me."

"Be safe," Jalil said backing the truck between two others already parked.

He liked Tommy. He really did but what frightened him was that he saw so much of himself in the boy. White or Black there was always that need in young men trying to aspire to achieve the world's riches with little or no patience. It almost inevitably ended in disaster but what is it they say about man learning most not on the mountaintop but more so when down in the valley. So, if this mad, reckless, scramble for wealth and riches to establish oneself as successful doesn't invariably end in death this may very readily turn into an epiphany of sorts. And I hoped it would for Tommy. He was a good boy, in search of, floundering helplessly and reaching for whoever would toss him a life jacket or lend a hand and I only wished someone had extended me a hand when I was his age. That's okay I was there for him now and for the past year I'd taken it on myself to talk to him every day about life. What I liked about Tommy was that he wasn't like most young people nowadays. Tommy listened and I knew I was having some type of affect when his mother dropped him off one morning a couple of months ago and came over to me and said—and I had never met the woman—'keep talking to Tommy. He's a good boy and he respects you. He talks about you every day. I'm sure he would have quit a long time ago if not for you Mr. Jalil. Just keep talking to him.' And then just like that she walked away with me never uttering a word.

As I drove home that day my thoughts returned to Tommy. He was a life worth saving. And I intended on doing just that although I knew it was time to give him that little extra push right through here I wasn't exactly sure how. Nonetheless I made it a point to stop by Queens College and pick up an application and some financial aid forms. I'd at least had the foresight to put away a little severance pay for myself as well as the girl's college tuition when I'd first gotten in the game and it made sense to pinch off just enough to make sure Tommy could go if that was his intent. But first we'd see how he responded to the suggestion that there was no time like the present. After all, tomorrow is promised no man.

The following morning I woke up late—well late for me anyway—and if it weren't for Theresa would have forgotten the application.

"Thank you baby," I said kissing her and the girls goodbye.

"Arriving at work that day the old man was out in the yard. Jalil joined the small crowd gathered around him.

"I have some very disturbing news this morning. Tommy Minola was gunned down last night in an apparent robbery attempt," the old man said as the application fell to the ground from Jalil's hands.

Red, White, & Boo

Or

Do Black Lives Really Matter

I no longer count the Black men and women who have tragically died at the hands of law enforcement or other white supremacist groups over the past year. And though I have a problem with labeling law enforcement in the same breath as many of the racist white groups who have declared war on African Americans I must say that too many, (one is too many), African Americans have been killed by the hands of law enforcement to simply overlook the fact that racism is endemic and so woven into our society that many Americans outside of the African American community have come to rationalize that there is not a problem at all but simply a miscommunication between law enforcement and the African American community who have little or no respect for the law.

Contrary to this belief here is a question I'd like to pose to those Americans and law enforcement who continually espouse the idea that Blacks are miscreants who have absolutely no regard for the law. Since when I ask has American law enforcement also become judge and jury executing African Americans like Eric Garner for the heinous crime of selling loose cigarettes on the street? And yet the African American community grieves the loss of another Black man at the hands of law enforcement.

This week we saw the killing of Sandra Bland and a Cincinnati, Ohio man both for minor traffic stops and both of whom were unarmed and who proposed no threat to themselves or others. And yet they lay dead, murdered by law enforcement officers in the line of duty.

Several weeks ago, a nineteen year old white man went into a Charleston, South Carolina church and proceeded to take the lives of nine rather prominent members of the African American community under the auspices of the Confederate flag which in itself is symbolic of the South's dual society and the continued subjugation of the Negro under slavery. When all was said and done America was again in shock. I believe that I mentioned before that America leads the world in shock.

I continue to question how white America views this latest tragedy. Did these nine African Americans fall into the realm of outcasts and miscreants while attempting to meet in a place of worship and pray to God for renewed hope and strength?

How did white America view this latest tragedy? In my own distorted view white America saw this as a deviation from the American dream. In their eyes this was an abomination, a tragedy, a deviation by one misguided American youth and like law enforcement did not cast a pall over the entire community but was in large due to the Confederate flag which had long ago become a symbol of racism. So what was their reaction to this latest atrocity committed against an already disenfranchised segment of the American public? Their reaction was swift and conclusive. The problem arose from not the systemic racism so inherent in our country but the rallying cry posed by the Confederate flag. The answer they proposed was that the flag had to go. The flag had to be removed from the state house. Never have I seen legislation move so swiftly. This was the answer. In lieu of this, the flag was removed and still there were protests from the white community.

To too many of us, we already knew that the removal of the Confederate flag was a ploy, a distraction to diminish and quell the anger which by now is embedded within the African American psyche and waiting to explode as we have seen after the Eric Garner, Michael Brown, and the Freddie Gray lynching's as we watch another African American murdered at the hands of the authorities.

The removal of the flag however is not the real issue. With most issues there are causes and that is the real issue. America has yet to deal with the real issue. The real issue is racism and until we deal with it we will not and cannot create a viable solution. The flag is only symbolic of deeper problems; one that we as Americans are not yet ready to tackle or deal with.

And though I am a firm believer in the American political system as perhaps our best way to elicit change it has come to me after considerable thought and study that legislation cannot effect change in a people's mindset. And until there is dialogue and communication among Americans both Black and white it is not the Confederate flag which white supremacist groups hover around nor the American flag which law enforcement hovers around that are the problem

but the deeply entrenched systemic ills of racism that present the real problem.

The End of an Era

"Hey Shay! How you been man? I haven't heard from you in a month of Sundays. How are you doing man?"

"I'm good, Monique. You know I just started with Deuterman & Karney."

"That's right. You know I totally forgot. I didn't know what happened to you. I heard you talking about it but it totally slipped my mind. You told me you were considering taking the position but I didn't know you took it. So, how do you like it?"

"I love it. Right now it's a little overwhelming but it's okay. I'm in the office by eight and don't get home until somewhere around nine, nine-thirty. You know what I'm saying… But I don't mind. Right now I'm just sort of familiarizing myself with the way they do things. Like I said it's all a little overwhelming."

"Well, don't be discouraged. I know you Shay. Just remember Rome wasn't built in a day. And you know what they say. All work and no play makes Johnny a dull boy. Why don't you put the job on hold, step away from it and come out with us tonight? I think it'll be good for you."

"Sounds like a plan. Let me get off this phone and see how much of this work I can get done. Either way I'll let you know."

"Love you Shay."

"Love you more."

At six o'clock that evening Shay was no closer to seeing daylight than when he'd arrived that morning. This was the career chance of a lifetime and after only three years as a criminal attorney he hadn't lost a case. So, when Deuterman & Karney came a calling it wasn't a surprise.

At twenty eight he'd chosen a career he loved. Now he was beginning to reap the benefits. He'd started at the annual lawyer's salary but in three years he'd doubled it. And now he'd taken on this new challenge the same way he did every other challenge in his life. His need to succeed was only overshadowed by his fear of failure. But after three straight weeks of twelve hour days he knew Monique was right. He needed a break. He needed to get out.

Entering the club that night he'd glad he'd listened to Shay.

"Shay! What's up baby? Thought you fell off the edge of the earth man. Where've you been?"

"In transition. New job and all…"

"Well, you know your girl missed you. She ain't been the same without you."

Shay smiled and hugged Benny. He was home. They'd all grown up together and for the most part they'd all been fair to moderately successful. Shay called it the second Harlem Renaissance.

Benny was Shay's best friend and had been since second grade when Shay came to Benny's defense when Lil Blue Boy Johnson was whipping the tar out of Benny. They'd been inseparable ever since. Benny had graduated from NYU and become an accountant for some big firm downtown but soon found his heart wasn't in it and gone into real estate just when the Harlem Revitalization started grabbing several choice pieces of prime. At Monique and Shay's suggestion he'd opened Benny's the now popular upscale bar for the preppy, professional crowd.

"Whatcha having tonight? The usual?"

"Think I'm gonna keep it light. How about a glass of wine?"

"Coming up," Benny said pointing to the far end of the bar where Monique stood surrounding by a group of well attired businessmen.

"Hey lady," Shay said grabbing her and pulling her to him.

"Hey baby. Didn't know if you were going to make it or not."

"Not every day a guy gets asked out by a bright, beautiful, sister."

"Keep talking. I hear you."

Shay laughed.

"I missed you," Monique whispered in his ear. "I think we all missed you."

"Missed you too Moni," Shay said kissing Monique on the cheek when Benny walked up and handed Shay the glass of wine.

"You alright baby?" Benny said staring at Monique.

"Yeah, Benny. Why do you ask?"

"Cause you've been moping around ever since your boy got ghost."

"Oh, I have not," Monique said smiling her face beginning to blush.

"Looked to me like she was doing alright when I walked over," Shay said trying to put the young woman at ease. But Benny was not one to let up.

"Sometimes I think Mone just keeps a crowd around for comic relief. For her it's just idle banter but the brothers be dead serious."

"No, they're not. They're just looking for some good spirited conversation."

"And you certainly give them that. Had two in here earlier this week ready to go to blows because your girl here made 'em look silly."

Benny and Monique smiled thinking back two nights ago.

"I asked this Negro who he was voting for and he said he was thinking about Hillary but he definitely wasn't voting for Romney. When he said that I went to the other end of the bar but Monique went on to read him the riot act then gave him a history of the Negro in the United States before telling him that she and most of the brothers and sisters in Benny's only frequented the place to engage in intelligent conversation and if he came he needed to come correct or not come at all. I mean they really got into it. When she got finished with him he drew back like he was going to swing on someone and four or five six brothers was on him."

"You don't have to tell me. Remember I used to room with her. And you don't know how many times I risked my life."

"You two need to stop," Monique said grinning as she sipped her Perrier.

"I watched my moms and my grandmother grow old gracefully and though they were both church going women they had mouths that handled things," Shay smiled. "And as they grew older there were no boundaries. They'd cut you to pieces with their words. Believe me brother you didn't want that to happen to you,"

"I hear you."

"The one commonality between the two was that age had somehow given them the right to speak freely. It was like over the years they had somehow earned the right. I think Mone here feels she has that same sort of entitlement and what can I say? She worked hard to be one of the brightest most intellectual Black woman I know and believe me I'm in touch with some of the sharpest minds you wanna know. So, why should she waste her time with some stupid, uninformed, wanna be Negro. It's like this. Put your time in, do your homework then you can step to me and we can go toe-to-toe but don't step to me if you're not ready cause all you're really looking for is an intellectual beat down. You feel me?"

"You know I feel you," Benny said nodding up and down.

A tall disheveled but distinguished fellow with a large, black and gray afro and goatee approached.

"Ladies. Gentlemen," he said grinning broadly.

"Gil, it's good to see you. How've you been?" Shay said grabbing the man's hand and pulling him forward in a hug.

"I'm good. Teaching an English class up at Columbia. Trying to start writing again. You know. Same ol' same ol'. Did you see the debate last night?"

"I'm still trying to figure it out," Mone said sipping from her stirrer.

"Ya gotta be careful at who and what you listen to and make sure you keep a fair amount of skepticism when you listen to both CNN and the candidates," Benny commented.

"And that's exactly why I'm still trying to figure it out. CNN was the promoter and they're obviously liberal democrats and I do think they're about promoting the most capable and viable candidate but they also have a vested interest," Mone said still sipping her drink.

"They're interest is the same interest as any other conglomerate. Money. And how do you make money? Ratings." Shay commented.

"But the whole build up, and all the publicity prior to seemed better than the debate itself if you ask me. I think I sat through the first hour in anticipation of something great about to happen. I was waiting for one of the candidates to give me the same type of hope Obama gave us when he was running. It didn't happen. Granted I got a chance to view them all and get to know them better than I had before but when it was over I still didn't know them or what they really stood for. It just seemed like a whole lot of posturing to me."

"Posturing and pandering. They were so busy not trying to step on each other's toes that they really couldn't expound on their beliefs and platforms."

"If they had any. Like I said it was a lot of posturing. Hillary as the frontrunner wasn't going to get into it with any of the other candidates. All she was trying to do was smile and look pretty and maintain her lead. She had nothing at stake and everything to lose."

"That's true," Shay commented. "As we used to say back in the day, 'the competition is none'. Her only dilemma is trying to convince Americans that she is honest and trustworthy. Ol' girl is still trying to live down the scandals that went on with her husband. Bill was a mess. Remember there was Whitewater, then the whole Monica Lewinsky charade, followed by I didn't inhale. Bill was a trip."

"That's so true," Gil laughed. "Bill was the man that did not. I did not have sex with that woman. I smoked but I did not inhale."

"I smoked but I did not inhale," Mone laughed. "And there's no doubt she blundered big time in the Benghazi case but over the last twenty to twenty-five years she's performed admirably in lieu of what she had to go through. She's really not the one to blame. Her husband is the one that gave the Clinton's a bad name."

"I couldn't agree more but she still comes off as cold and calculating if you ask me. Everything she says and does seems cold and calculated almost contrived. I keep trying to get a feel for her but for some reason I just can't. I got a feel for Bill with all his faults and indiscretions but when it comes to Hillary I feel nothing. It may have something to do with the way she ran her last campaign against Barack."

"She was something there wasn't she. Both she and Bill had a take no prisoners' policy and went after Obama with everything they had didn't they?" Benny said.

"Barack was cool though. He took the high road and refused to get down in the mud with her. He refused to mudsling or get get grimy and gully. He didn't have to. He had a vision and a plan. Unlike Hillary it wasn't just about the power that comes with holding the highest office in the land."

"And he kicked it in the ass didn't he without so much as a bad word or scandal in the eight years he's been in office," Gil said the pride glowing.

"He embodies the whole American value system better than those that constructed it. He has returned America to what Republicans consider the good ol' days," Benny said.

"No, Benny I wouldn't say that. I think what Republicans refer to as the good ol' days is quite different. I think what Republicans refer to as the good ol' days is the pre-Civil Rights years when they were in control and segregation was rampant when they had an air of superiority and we were second class citizens," Shay said.

"Don't get it twisted my brother. We're still second class citizens." Mone interrupted.

"You're right. But I think what Barack did was more a testament to the man and his character. Aside from the political successes he had he restored the dignity and pomp to the White House and the office of the presidency. Just the fact that he portrays a good strong Black man in a time when we are portrayed as anything but good strong Black man is a tribute to the man."

"Ain't that the truth. It's funny you say that. I never thought of it that way," Mone said looking into Shay's eyes.

"Why would you being a woman? Why would you concern yourself with the way the brothers are portrayed and depicted in America's eye?"

"Don't even try to play me Shay. I'm quite aware of how brothers' are treated and stereotyped. I just hadn't really considered how big the role Obama's had on negating the negativity of it all."

"People don't look at Obama as a man but only as the president. But the image he portrays hasn't really been seen since the likes of King and X and it's coming at a time when we so sorely need it." Shay continued.

"So, who's his successor going to be," Mone queried.

"I have to agree with Shay. Hillary may be our only option but she doesn't really get it done for me. I think the best thing about her is the fact that Bill will advise her and will not allow her to fail. There are only a few candidates that I can remember that has had such a plethora of knowledge of the office going in. Perhaps the only president in recent history that's had such an advantage is Bush and I think that he was such an egotist that he probably ignored his father's advice in lieu of making a name for himself."

"And I guess that's what makes her our only and best choice." Mone interjected.

"So, you're writing off the new kid, Bernie Sanders?" Gil said in that way of his way that kept us on our toes, cognizant and open.

"By no means. I think Bernie's got some interesting ideas and I think what is appealing to many Americans right through here is that they've watched Washington politics and the logjam that has arisen out of partisan politics. They've seen legislation reach an impasse at every turn in reaction to Obama being in office and their both frustrated and disappointed in Washington politics. And I may be going out on a limb but Obama has achieved marked success despite being the first Black president and this being the most unproductive congress in the history of this country. I'm thinking there could be a correlation?" Benny mused.

"Bernie presents a different type of candidate. He's almost Trump like in a sense. Like Trump he's attracting those Americans that are fed up with Washington politics. He reminds me of Trump in that he's attracting those voters that have basically had it with a Washington that can't get anything done but he also reminds me of Barack in a sense that he's not your typical politician. He's radical in his ideas and philosophies for the future of America. He has a vision for the country.

It's funny though—what is he seventy four and the oldest candidate—and he's still the most progressive by far. Bernie's talking about things like democratic socialism and a redistribution of the wealth. His whole platform speaks of the one per cent of the population controlling ninety per cent of the country's wealth. He deems it unfair in lieu of the poverty levels among Blacks and other minorities. His thinking along these lines are radical and I can feel his passion. I like him and although he's raising millions of dollars and bringing out record numbers of crowds Black folks have no idea who he is. But the way he's exploded onto the scene by next year he promises to pose a real threat to Hillary and don't let Blacks get the idea that he's included them by name as part of his agenda.

Right now he's doing and saying things that Barack couldn't say. If you remember when Barack was campaigning we kept asking why Barack wouldn't identify with us specifically. He couldn't. By identifying us he would have been saying or looking at us as a special interest group that he was forced to defer to because of his own lineage. Instead he referred to the welfare of all Americans and I must say a lot of us felt somewhat dejected. But Bernie not being the first anything can build a platform on the poor and disenfranchised and can single us out by race and nationality and expose the inequalities with no repercussions." Shay stated matter-of-factly.

"Let's see how that works for him. And don't get me wrong I both like and respect his candidness but he frightens the hell out of me. I remember when Bush was in office and went to the grocery store and didn't know what a scanner was and the media jumped all over him saying he was out of touch. I just wonder how in touch Bernie is coming out of an all white state like Vermont calling himself a socialist and threatening to redistribute America's wealth and to top it off by mentioning aid for poor Black folks." Gil stated.

"If you ask me that's a signature for suicide."

"But then on the other he differs from most of the other Democrats because he's against gun control claiming that as American's he doesn't want to amend the Second Amendment which is a dichotomy if you ask me. With young Black males dying every day in urban areas across the country from guns how can you say you are a proponent for the plight of the poor and impoverished and scream that Black Lives Matter and yet be for the right of every American to own and carry a firearm. Seems ludicrous to me..."

"What scares me even more about Bernie is that he's not a student of American history. These things which he proposes are tantamount to treason. What he's proposing is suicidal. History shows us this in more than one example." Benny said.

"So if I may ask in closing 'cause I've gotta run who are you three going to vote for?" Gil asked as he gathered his belongings.

"To tell you the truth Professor Gil I'm not exactly sure," Benny said clearing the table.

"After this discussion I'm going to have to say the jury's still out," Mone added.

"And you Shay?"

"All I'm going to say is that Obama will be sorely be missed. Come on Mone. Let me walk you home."

The Rumor

At twenty two she was on her way. It wouldn't be long now. They couldn't pigeonhole or stereotype her. She'd followed daddy's plan to a tee and graduated Bennett College Magna Cum Laude. Yes, she was on her way now. She'd taken a year off after graduation to reassess her life after Shamir had walked out of her life.

College hadn't been easy for her. She'd double majored in English and History as an undergraduate with the hopes of studying law and becoming a lawyer. Most days she spent in her five by nine dorm room or the college library her head deep in some book.

About the only semblance of normal campus life she had were the daily visits from Shamir. At six foot three and a starter on A & T's basketball team Shamir Nelson was the heartthrob of most of the girls at A & T and Bennett. Charcoal black with long black dreads he could have had any of the thousands of young ladies but he had chosen her.

An engineering major Shamir wasn't like most of the young men she'd had a chance to meet on campus. He was older, more mature. Most of the other guys didn't seem to know what they were there for. There were those that were there simply to say they were going to college because mommy and daddy said it was the right thing to do.

They came from good homes but had yet to see the light. Then there were those that seemed to be enrolled for no other reason than to party and get high. They were a dime a dozen. But Shamir was different. He seemed to know. He had a plan. His life had been well-planned out.

Now there's always been a certain stereotype about preacher's kids being different. And I guess this was true of Shamir. Quiet and unassuming, he had plans. Majoring in engineering he worked as hard if not harder than I did. And I liked the fact that as a sophomore he'd already contacted several Fortune five hundred companies with the hopes of doing a summer internship with one. It was the first time we'd been separated since we'd met the year before. And Lord knows did I suffer from separation anxiety. I mean outside of my little high school affairs which usually didn't last more than a week Shamir was the first guy with whom I ever had a serious relationship.

I met him in one of my history classes. I think it was Aldoph Hitler's The Third Reich or something like that. We had to watch something on Hitler's Germany—you know one of those PBS things where the Gestapo are marching all loud and heavy footed through a ravaged, war torn Germany—when Shamir decided it was time to introduce his fine self to me.

In the weeks that followed I spent every spare minute moment I could find with Shamir. We didn't do anything special. He'd pick me up and we'd go to the caf together or to the library to study. When basketball season started I'd go to his games at least the ones at home. I mean we did everything together. Sometimes we'd just hold

hands and walk and talk. For the first time in my life I knew what falling in love was. He wasn't like any other guy I knew. I trusted him.

A month or two later I gave myself to him. It was my first time and though I had had my trepidations about sleeping with someone before I was married it was okay. Sometimes I'd be with him and he'd looked at me my and whole body would tingle all over kinda of like when you get the heebie-jeebies but this was in a good way. And the times he would touch me or take me in his arms to kiss me I would literally melt. That's what my baby Shamir used to do me. I get a lil' teary-eyed even thinking about him now.

We had been together for the better part of a year when basketball season ended and they were throwing propositions at him left and right about playing overseas or even possibly in the NBA but they didn't know my baby. He wasn't in the least bit interested in playing professional ball. That's why I say he was a typical pk and as everyone knows preacher's kids are different. And though the ones I have met certainly fit the stereotype and are strange in some ways Shamir was no different. He was just strange in a different kind of way. I mean like what little Black boy wouldn't have died and gone to heaven at just the thought of playing ball overseas or in the NBA but not Shamir.

All he'd ever wanted to do was be an engineer and it didn't dawn on me until the end of his junior year when he started searching the job market in the Maryland, D.C. area was the first time since I met him that I had the sudden realization that his plans didn't necessarily involve me. Prior to his graduation—he was a year ahead of me—I'd begun hearing rumors that he was creepin' on the yard. You know going to other girl's dorms when lights were out. I didn't pay much mind to it as the girls from A & T were always talking about us or stating some shit around us being African American princesses because we went to the prestigious all-girl's college across the street. I chalked it up to jealousy and ignored the rumors 'cause my man took good care of me and what he did in his spare time was his own business. But mostly I disregarded it because I had a hard time believing Shamir could not possibly been seeing anyone when he spent twenty three of the twenty four hours in a day either with me or on the phone with me.

When he graduated my parents and my older brother were the ones that drove up and helped him move to Silver Springs. I returned to school for my senior year and it was much the way I started. Alone.

Still, he called me every night when he got home from work. He loved it. He loved the job, his first apartment, his independence; everything and I must admit I was happy for him. And each time I talked he'd tell me how I had to come.

"You'll love it baby. There's so much to do. I met some Q's up here and they've taken me everywhere. And the nightlife. OMG!!"

"I can't wait to join you baby," was all I could muster so torn was my heart with the grief of loneliness.

That last year, my senior year seemed to drag on forever. No matter what I did I couldn't make the days go by any faster. Hour and a half classes now seemed like three hour classes. I even started going out with my sorority sisters hoping that if I were involved I wouldn't just sit and pine away thinking about Shamir but that didn't help either.

"What's wrong with you girl? I invited you out so I wouldn't have to be the one to write your obituary. I already have two term papers due. That would just be another unwanted writing assignment. I'd be hard pressed to find any of your positive attributes. Seriously though, you have got to stop sitting around moping over this fool. Shamir ain't no more thinking about you than a man on the moon. He up in D.C. making good money and partying with the rest of them ho-mongering Q dogs. You can best believe that he ain't mopin' around thinking about you girlfriend. You betta get on out there and finds you someone that means you some good. At least for the night..." Ebony said walking away as my sorors fell out laughing.

I don't know why they didn't get it. Everyone wasn't out to get their itch scratched by just anyone. To some of us things ran a lot deeper. That's why Shamir and

I were different. Sure we slept together and it was damn good. Something you wanted to write home and tell your mama about but it was more, so much more than making sure my eyelashes were on fleek or measuring a niggas worth by how many orgasms could I achieve in a night, how much money he had in his pocket and what kind of whip he had. No. What they didn't realize was that Shamir had more than that. We were friends and no matter what they said I trusted him. He was the only man I'd ever been with heart, soul and body. He was the first and if I had anything to do with it he would be my last.

And he was. A week later he called me and told me to have myself tested. He was HIV positive.

Purple and Grape

"All I find I keep," was all the tall Black man hooded man said sticking the gun in my side.

"Brother, I just finished putting in eight hours for the man six days outta the last seven days. You have to be outta your fuckin' mind if you believe I'm going to give you shit," I was never more serious. This nigga would have to kill me first.

"Niggas dying out here everyday. I don't give a fuck. Now give up the cash."

I turned to face him. He didn't seem to be a bad brother just a brother like a whole lotta brothers that had fallen on bad times.

"C'mon brother let me buy you a shot and we'll talk about it."

"Nigga is you kiddin' me. I can buy myself my own shot when you empty your pockets," he said the boldness leaving his voice.

"I ain't givin' you shit and if you shoot me you're not only gonna have me on your conscience but the cops on your ass and for what a couple of hundred dollars? Then you gonna be runnin' for the rest of your life. And like I said for what—a couple of hundred dollars—be for real. Come on let's go grab a couple of beers."

Somehow I must've gotten through and minutes later we were making our way down 8th Avenue towards Small's.

All the usual folks were there for happy hour.

"What up Stretch?"

"I'm good?"

"How you doing Blue? You certainly looking like everything is going your way."

"I try," she said knowing she was looking just as good as she wanted to. I'd always meant to follow up with her and to this day don't know why I hadn't. "Who's your friend?"

I hadn't had a chance to get my boys name. It wasn't as if we'd met at a meet and greet over wine.

"Go ahead man. Introduce yourself while I head to the little boy's room," I said taking my leave.

When I returned the two were engrossed in what seemed a rather lively conversation.

"I like your friend Sharif. He has some interesting ideas on a number of issues," Blue said smiling.

Yeah. His issues had me wanting to beat him down on the one hand and thanking God I wasn't in his shoes on the other.

"You said Sharif has some interesting views. Care to expound? I'd like to hear his views on Black-on-Black crime in the ghetto," I said eyeing him closely.

"Oh, that's just so trite, so mundane. His ideas—at least the ones he's shared with me—are so fresh and provocative. Why would you want to speak of something so trite? What intelligent Black man even thinks there is a need for conversation when it comes to that?"

"Nonetheless I'd like to hear Mr. Sharif's views," I said my eyes never leaving the brother's face. I think you'd find Mr. Sharif's views on Black-on-Black crime may surprise you."

"What you asking me brother? You asking me if I would stick up another Black man to feed my daughter? If that's the question you're asking me then you already know. Would I commit a crime for that same little Black girl. Hell yeah."

I smiled looking over at Blue who was shaken by his words.

"You're adamant in your ignorance, Sharif," I said ordering another round.

"Adamant only in your world. My world's a whole lot different baby and the only thing that's ignorant is that you have taken on a culture in which you see yourself as being bout it bout it and have bought into a system that defiles, denigrates, degrades, debases, disparages you then when you serve no other purpose it dismisses you and sends you to and makes you a ward of the Department of Corrections. That's my world.

You play chess man? If you did you'd see that they—the powers that be—have you in check. But then again you probably wouldn't even recognize that you're no more than a pawn in the whole scheme of things in the game of life my brother. You have not come to recognize that though have you?" Sharif laughed. "You can't because although your body's free your mind is still in shackles. Look at you in your Jos A Banks suit."

"Armani," I corrected.

"Exactly what I'm talking about. Look at you quoting the name of someone you've never met. Yet, you're running around like you're a moving billboard wearing his name on your back. Brother you're exactly the Negro Malcolm was talking about when he said…

"Oh, and I say it again, you've been had. You've been took. You've been hoodwinked. Bamboozled. Led astray. Run amok!"

He's talking about you my brother," Sharif concluded. You have no knowledge of self. You have bought into his identity. You have let him brainwash you into what it is that he wants you to be. He has defined you my brother."

"What do you mean Sharif? You're losing me. Stretch has not been brainwashed. If anything he's one of the clearest thinks I know. I don't know how long you've known him but you're not going to find a better bother. He's decent. He ain't tryna be down with nothin' or nobody. He's a rare find nowadays. He's one of the few brothers that defines himself and the road he travels. And to top that he does it with a bit of flair and he's a gentleman. You don't find that nowadays. Tell me something Sharif? How long have you known Stretch?"

Sharif smiled.

"I have to admit that I just met the brother."

"And he's buying you drinks and you're hatin' on him like that? Is there something I missed?"

"Yeah. There's quite a bit you missed Blue but let's put that on hold for the moment. The fact of the matter is your man Shariff uses the term brother so freely and loosely that I half-way want to believe we are but anytime you treat your brother with less than the dignity he deserves you can't be considered a brother of mine."

"When I use the term brother I am only endearing myself to you so we can sit and converse. It does not mean I accept you into my clan. If you speak English and live in America and I speak Spanish and live in Spain we would have a hard time communicating. Therefore we could not be brothers culturally because we do not speak the same language and have little shared experience. I am sorry to say but we live in two different worlds. It is no different here in Harlem. I have white neighbors who live next door that do not speak to me because they do not what to say. They know that their interests are not mine and I know that mine are not theirs. And that's okay and I accept that but what bothers me more is that there are too many brothers like you Stretch. There are too many brothers that move up to Harlem because nowadays it's the trendy thing to do. We do share the same experiences but instead of acknowledging the experiences we shared as a people you and your kind try to act as if it never existed. Are you ashamed of who you are and where you come from?"

"Aren't you making a lot of accusations considering you don't know this man? Did you know that he attended Howard University, an historically Black university?"

Shariff laughed again.

"Whoa! Slow down sister. Stretch is a big boy. He can defend himself. Why are you being so overprotective anyway?"

"Cause its happy hour. And we come here damn near every night to laugh, and talk and unwind and put the day behind us. We don't come here to criticize and hate on each other."

"It's no more than two supposedly strong Black men from different sides of the track sharing our experiences. No harm in that is there?"

"You're the only one talking. I don't get the sharing part."

"I'm sure when I finish my little soliloquy Stretch will say his part," Sharif said smiling at Blue before finishing off the glass.

"Let him finish Blue. I'm curious as to where he's going with this."

"We walk the same streets everyday and we are as far apart as the moon and the sky and do you know why?"

"Please continue," Stretch said.

"Well there are many reasons but the primary reason is because what Carter G. Woodson so aptly named his book. It is because of the miseducation of the Negro. The first thing he did was to place himself in our lives as master. When he assumed this position he made us understand very quickly that we were no longer required to think. Instead he would do the thinking for us. And so for the first two hundred years in this country all choices and decisions were made for us by the master. Reading would increase thought and make a Negro say 'what if' so books were forgiven. And being that we were unable to think and because it was easier not to think we listened and we did what the master said even if what is we were doing for us was detrimental to our very lives.

Nothing's changed except that he has perfected the miseducation of the Negro to the extent that we are lost in the need for upward mobility with no clear end plan in sight."

"Oh my God. Are you telling me the quest for upward mobility is a bad thing?"

"By no means Blue. Upward mobility is a beautiful thing taken in the right context. Don't get me wrong."

"And what is the right context?" Blue asked.

"That's a good question and one that so many of us got wrong following the Civil Rights Movement. There's a good reason why we are in such a precarious situation today. We took Dr. King's message of respect and equality to mean material equality and in our haste to be seen as Americans equal in all respect we lost sight of everything. We who had been the purveyors of knowledge within our segregated communities now saw the edifice of tall buildings as improvement. But it was the indoctrination of our minds that so bothered me. We fought saying the pledge of allegiance because we did not consider ourselves a part of this non-United States of America but we did not recognize all the other ways in which we were hoodwinked and bamboozled. We bought into the idea that upward mobility simply meant amassing wealth and material items. At the same time a people without roots and without a culture can be shaped, molded and shaped. There is no reference point to look back on for clarification. There is no governing body, no guidance, no law of the land. There is no Moses on the mountain with the tablet containing the Ten Commandments.

Oh, there was Dr. King and Malcolm and a host of others our young people will never come to know because they have been dissuaded from searching for the truth or coming to know themselves and whence they come. And as you and I both know if you cut off the head you kill he body. This wasn't by accident. And once there was no one to guide you. It became leadership by proxy and came in so many forms. But one of the most devastating ways it was employed was by the media. Your utilitarianism suddenly became a priority. You may not have been able to serve in the First World War but you can serve the needs of this country now in so many ways. And since they have taken over the ways in which they not teach but indoctrinate us into being malleable misfits and miscreants we are still shackled. They have taken our will to think and somehow indoctrinated us to simply react instead making us some kin to Piaget's dogs that simply replied to stimuli. That is who we have become. This is our evolution.

Now our children who are in such dire need of love and guidance and education have been turned over, relinquished to the very same man who enslaved our bodies so that he can now enslave our mind while we go in search of another dollar.

Black parents have left their children in the midst of the enemy that has raped and lynched them since for generations and asked them to educate them. Our children! Our most precious resources! Why niggas you have lost your minds. So, nowadays if you ask a thirteen year old who Nat Turner or even Joe Biden is they have no idea. But they can tell you what the number thirteen looks like when it comes to a pair of Nike Jordans.

And you're no better walking around mindless talkin' about in your Armani suit. What are you doing?"

"What do mean what am I doing?"

"Our parents taught me as well as anyone within earshot that we had a responsibility to ourselves as well as every other Black person that once we got up out of the muck and mire to pull the ext Negro out but we can only lead if we know whence we come from and who we followed. We have always followed men of great being, great intellect, and wisdom and they have led us from despair to hope of a new day. And never has that man been compromised or been able to be bought out by a shiny suit and a fancy car. But now our sights have been shifted and our focus changed. And in the process we've lost our identity, our moral turpitude and have been assimilated, acculturating his mongrel culture whose god is capitalism and who will do anything for it. That is who I see when I see you in your Armani suit and Italian loafers.

Upward mobility does not mean we simply imitate white folks buying patterns. Upward mobility doesn't mean neglecting our children to purchase a Benz or Audi or that home with the two car garage and abandon our children to make time and a half. Upward mobility does not mean turning our children over to their network programming which tells them that they need this and that at fifteen minute intervals yet not giving them the smarts or the critical thinking skills to differentiate between what they need and what Madison Avenue insists they must have to keep up with the rest of the boys and girls in America.

Have you ever taken a look at our children today?"

"I'll agree they are nothing to be proud of," Blue admitted.

"No. I mean have you ever looked at our kids on a purely superficial level?"

"I'm not sure I know what you mean."

"I'm talking about the way they dress, the way they talk. Here you are in money making Manhattan the center of capitalism for the world. You have Madison Avenue prescribing what we wear, how we dress. Move over to Fashion Avenue wear these clothes are first put on the streets of America. We are the center but isn't it funny that in a matter of weeks these poor urban kids that can't see their way out of the city are imitated across America."

"You do have a point."

"I know I do. Our kids are on the front lines and we are not doing anything about it. We have become so selfish with our own desires that we have forgotten our children. So, instead of us teaching them and securing the real upward mobility, that is the teaching of our children about things that are truly relevant such as our history, and the way in which we treat ourselves and our fellow man we leave them instead to the networks and their depictions of us which we now use to define us. It's truly heart rendering and yet we are so busy seeking acceptance and waiting to say we made it that we've forgotten what it is that is important to us."

"And what is it that's important to us since you're the spokesperson for all Black people?"

"Listen, I don't pretend to be a spokesperson for all Black people. All I try to do is be educated, aware and conscious of how I live my life and what it means to be a strong, intelligent, Black man in today's world. If I can do that then I can at least present a positive Black role model to today's America. I can only do what I can do in my current position but I can be the best of in whatever role He gives me.

But I am aware which is why I don't champion goods from the country that still has the majority of us locked up in mental slavery.

Here. Let me give you an example of what I'm talking about. Back in the day when Nike first came out they were like any other startup company struggling to get along. At the same time Michael Jordan was a young player just starting to make a name for himself when Philip Knight the founder of Nike decided to give Mike a call. The rest is history.

Michael went on to become the greatest player to ever play the game. Nike rode Michael's coattails and went on to become one of the biggest companies in the world.

Mike got a stipend in relation to what Nike made because his face was the forefront for the company. Now kids who have no education, no marketable skills and can't scrape two nickels together to make a dime suddenly feel compelled to run out and buy a pair of two hundred dollar sneakers. If their mommy's and daddy's don't buy them they feel no remorse for robbing or stealing them.

They've been so inundated and programmed by capitalism. I bought some New Era caps awhile back to resale and was riding with a friend of mine's son one day. When he opened the box the kid lost his mind. Started telling me that they were 'official snapbacks'. I asked him what makes them official. He couldn't tell me that or what separated them from the old snapback that my daddy used to wear to cut the grass. He couldn't tell me but he wanted to buy the same cap that my father used to pay a dollar for. Only now it had a company logo on it which made it 'official' and sold for forty dollars.

He was typical. He had the beginnings of dreadlocks which was all the latest fad and a Bob Marley t-shirt on. Now I grew up with Bob Marley and considered him—as many did—a prophet and so with the combination of hair do and shirt on I was curious as to why he donned both. He, however, didn't have a clue as to who the man was he wore on the front of his shirt or what his dreads represented. He knew nothing more than it was the latest style donned by other teens his age. In other words it was the latest fashion. Funny thing though, his mother who graduated Magna Cum Laude from a most prestigious university in the northeast would sit down at night and twist his hair for him and at other times would send him to her beauty parlor at other times to have his hair done had never questioned either his choice of hair dos or his wearing of the Marley shirt. She had never considered asking him why he made the choices he did. In other words, he received no other information than what the media and his peers had given him and so he wore the hair do and shirt with no other information other than that it was popular."

"Shariff, why are you telling us all this? I mean really. I get all that. But why are you telling us all this? It's no different with white kids who wear swastikas and Confederate flags and shoot nine innocent churchgoers in Charlestown, South Carolina. I just heard an interview by jazz trumpeter Branford Marsalis where he said that teenagers don't act they react. In other words teenagers don't think they simply react to the stimuli presented them." Blue said.

"My point exactly. And I have no problem with that. My problem is that we are not white folks. And we as Black folks have an obligation not only to ourselves but to our children to be equipped with the knowledge and baton to pick up the struggle ad lead us into the next generation. We all come into this world as a blank slate. It is up to us as Black folks, as parents to do what our parents did for us. We do not need another Michael Brown, Freddie Gray or Eric Garner to wake us from our malaise. It is not at these times that we should be shocked but if we know the history of our people in this country then there is no way we should be shocked. We do not have the luxury of looking at President Obama and acknowledge that we have somehow made it as a people. No. We should see Obama for what he is. An anomaly... But he is in no way representative of all Black folks in America; the majority of whom remain poor and uneducated. We can be extremely proud that he has risen to the heights that he has. It is instead, our job, our responsibility to pick up Dr. King's mantle and repair the disconnect that has purposely been put in place to sow the chords of discontent. No longer is it sufficient to simply rest on the laurels of our president and say that since he's in the White House that we have made it as a people. This is simply not true. I'm not sure if it's social media or just the media in general but I can't remember seeing this many Black men being killed by cops in my lifetime as I've seen under his watch. The fact is we have not arrived. But Black folks are easily pacified and are under the impression that we have finally arrived."

"And so you are angry at the world and you believe that because you feel this way that we have as a people lost focus?"

"I do."

"And what may I ask makes you different than me," I asked.

"It depends on whose eyes and perception I am viewed from. From a bigoted white cops point of view there is little or difference between you and I. But does it matter how he perceives me? Not in the least. I cannot try to work on him and work on me as well. Life is too short. But what I can do is resolve to stay both educated, informed so that I can avoid all confrontations with him and know how to diffuse a situation which favors him and not because of his superior intellect but simply because he has a gun and no regard for my life. I just believe it is our job to teach and address our children around the systemic pitfalls designed towards the genocide of Black men. I simply believe that if equip our young men with their history in this great country of ours and all that we have had to overcome and continue to teach and educate them and try to help them to understand we could lessen so many of the obstacles put in place to maim and limit their overall growth. Education is the key and I'm not speaking of formal education per se. I am speaking of the education of a man such as yourself that has in some ways mastered this America dilemma that looks to eradicate us all which we know as racism.

This is our responsibility. We are supposed to educate our young men who are not aware that the drug trade so glamorized by Pacino in Scarface is not an avenue out of poverty but a means of keeping you in. You must teach him that this is film and not reality. In reality, the drug trade is a means of putting you in the system and keeping the unemployment statistics down. With drugs comes guns, more crime and the elimination of stable family units. That's only from our perspective.

However, from their perspective it keeps unemployment down. Just think of how many jobs are secured every time a young Black man is arrested for intent to sell and distribute.

There are the police, social services, emergency care, hospitals, social services, the judicial system and the prison system. We're in the drug trade with this Horatio Algers dream of going from rags to riches in a day and that just doesn't happen that way but again the media started with this introduction as an avenue to a life of glamour and wealth in the late seventies and he early eighties with the dawn of Superfly and Scarface.

And with no guidance and unable to think we actually looked at it as a viable way to eradicate poverty and other ills that plagued us."

"Okay. I've heard enough my brother. And I must agree with you whole heartedly. But I don't think you can arbitrarily pick people and make allegations because they don't dress like you.

I don't dress like you because there was a strong Black man in my life and he taught me everything you say that our young men need to be taught. I remember back in the sixties when the Panthers and other groups wore afros and dashikis. They were my heroes and I had the utmost respect for them but I wasn't going to don the clothing that white folks saw as the apparel of the defiant and rebellious. I understood but I could neither feed my son or educate him if I were in a five by eight cell so I wore that which was less confrontational only to stay one step ahead of the powers that be. If you know which group he's targeting I think it smart that you take the bulls eye off your back.

Still, I see no difference between you and me my brother so why target me? Know your enemy and know that I am not him. His aim is to divide and conquer. Our differences my brother is at subtle as the difference between purple and grape."

Cranberry Brown

Cranberry Brown couldn't have been more than eleven or twelve when mama first brought him home. I will never forget that day. It was a Tuesday in late November when I first met Cranberry Brown. Mama said she'd seen him diggin' through the dumpster lookin' for scraps of food in an alley off of St. Nicholas when she first approached him.

"Boy, what in the hell is you doing?" Mama yelled.

Somethin' akin to grits or porridge dripped from the sides of his mouth.

"He come 'round here near 'bout everyday Miss Ball. Just like some stray cat he do. He always diggin' through that dumpster. I watched him for a day or two. Now I puts a little somethin' out there when we gots leftovers. I believe he homeless or his mama just don't care. It's a shame how adults do their younguns nowadays. I would take him in but you know I gots six hungry mouths to feed already and can barely keep a roof over their heads."

"You ain't got to tell me Ms. Levy. All a us pretty much in the same boat," Mama replied grabbing the boy by the hand and pulling him along behind her.

"I don't where your mama is or why you eating out the dumpster but until I find out who you belong to you gonna stay with me and mines. It ain't much but we gots heat and we eat."

The boy said nothing staring at the big woman in amazement.

"You got a name boy?"

"My name is Cranberry. Cranberry Brown."

"Well, that's an odd name for a boy but I gots ta admit you're quite a handsome young man. We going to take you home and get you cleaned up and outta this cold. Get you a bath, into some clean clothes and get you somethin' on your stomach. I just hope Mimi got dinner ready.

"Where's your mama boy?"

"My name's Cranberry."

"I apologize," mama said smiling. "Where's your mama Cranberry?"

"I don't know. She left one day and said she was going to the store and she never came back."

"How long ago was that?"

"Close to a year now. December will be a year."

"So you been out here alone fending for yourself for close to a year?" Mama said in amazement.

"Yes ma'am."

"Did you go to the authorities to see if you could locate her?"

"What's the authorities?"

"Those are the police child."

"No, ma'am. Jojo said if I ask the police where mama is they'll send me away or lock me up."

"And who may I ask is Jojo?"

"He's my friend. We use to live in the same building and go to school together. We been in the same class since the first grade."

"That's not necessarily so Cranberry. The police would have turned you over to social services and they would have placed you in a children's shelter for a few weeks until they could place you with foster parents. It would have been better than searching through dumpsters for food. Look in my pocketbook and grab my keys."

Cranberry looked at the big woman and wondered why she was so trusting. They had just met and she hardly knew him. He was so stunned he just stood there.

"Hurry, Cranberry these bags are heavy." The boy's eye shifted from her warm, brown face to her pocketbook. Feeling her brown, leather, wallet his first instinct was to snatch it and head back down the stairs and into the street. As big as she was he knew getting away would be no problem but there was something about this woman that wouldn't allow him to. He wondered if he were getting soft. Finding the keys he held them up.

"It's the gold key. Go ahead. Sometimes it gets jammed so you have to jiggle it to get it in then turn it hard."

The boy did as he was told and stood back to let her enter. The woman was greeted by a host of children all hugging and kissing and talking at the same time vying for her attention. The big woman known as mama did her best to take it all in and respond to each one. When they were satisfied that she had taken care of all of their concerns she called them together. Cranberry counted four children. It sure seemed like more when they first came in but there were only four.

"Children, I'd like you to meet my friend Cranberry. Cranberry will be staying with us for awhile."

The two youngest who couldn't have been more than eight or nine looked at each other and burst out laughing.

"Cranberry? What kind of name is that for a kid?"

"What kind of name is Jeremiah?" shot a boy who appeared to be Cranberry's age. Cranberry liked him at once as the older boy stepped to his younger brother. "And since when do we laugh at a guest mama brings home? Now laugh again!" Jeremiah backed up knowing that his older brother was serious.

"Thank you Jonathan," mama said smiling at her oldest son. "Cranberry, this is my oldest son, Jonathan. And this is my daughter Mimi. You may wanna get in good with Mimi she is the best cook in the house. And these two laughing hyenas who have no manners or upbringing are my twins Jason and Jeremiah. Jeremiah I want you to get some clean blankets and pillow cases and make the spare bed up for Cranberry. Jason I want you to go and get a clean wash cloth, towel and toothbrush for Cranberry. Jonathan you and my friend look to be about the same size. See if you can find some pajamas for him to put on and an outfit for him to wear to school tomorrow."

"Yes, ma'am," Jonathan said smiling at the possibility of a new friend right here under the same roof. He was turning fourteen in a week or so and the twins were too young and silly for him. And Mimi—well—Mimi was a girl but Raspberry or whatever his name was looked to be his age and the possibilities seemed endless. Tomorrow he would introduce him to the fellas as his cousin or long lost brother. He wasn't sure yet. But what he was sure of was that Berry and he would run the building. He had a new best friend.

Once the boy had gone to take his bath and Mimi and mama were alone Mimi cornered her mother.

"Who is he ma?"

"Your guess is as good as mine sweetheart. I caught him eating out of the dumpster by Miss Levy's off of St. Nick and just grabbed him and brought him home."

"So, you don't know anything about him. Where's his parents?"

"Where are yours?"

"Right here talking to me."

"I said parents. Where's your father?"

Mimi dropped her head.

"I don't know."

"I don't know either. But should you have to fend for yourself because he doesn't want to be bothered?"

"No, I guess not."

"And neither should this child. It's too cold for a twelve year old to be out there hungry and homeless because some adult doesn't want to own up and take responsibility for what they brought into the world."

"But ma you don't know nothing about him. He could be a robber, a thief, a murderer anything. You don't know anything about him."

"I know that he's a child and no child should be out there on his own. Put yourself in his place and ask yourself if you wouldn't want someone to show you some love and compassion."

"I guess you're right. Let me go hide my pocketbook," Mimi said only half joking and ducking as mama swatted at her with the dish towel.

Mimi laughed and began to set the dining room table for dinner along with her mother's help when the boys appeared.

"Did you make his bed Jeremiah?"

"Yes, ma'am."

"And you didn't just throw the covers on top of it?"

"No, ma'am. I made it nice and neat just like you showed me."

"And what did you say to yourself when you were making it?"

"When there's a task at hand no matter how small do it grand or not at all," the young boy grinned as he repeated the catchy phrase mama had ingrained in them all.

"Come here sweetie," she said to Jeremiah who approached cautiously only to be smothered in hugs and kisses by the burly woman. The boy grinned and yelped and did his best to pull away.

"Jonathan," she said never looking up as she folded the napkins and placed them next to each plate before putting a fork, knife and spoon on top of each place setting.

"Yes ma'am."

"I don't know where they're going to place Cranberry when I take him to enroll him tomorrow but wherever they place him I want you to look after him and make sure no one bothers him or gives him a hard time. I don't want any of those little roughnecks picking at him or giving him a hard time because he's new. Don't want him getting into any fights or getting off on the wrong foot."

"No problem ma'am. You know I got him."

"No one's gonna bother me ma'am. I can take care of myself," Cranberry said walking in and having a seat in the living room next to Jonathan.

Mama never looked up from setting the table.

"And I'm sure you can sir. But being that you're new chances are someone's gonna try you and being that Jonathan's an honor roll student and stays out of trouble then please let him handle it for the first couple of months 'til the teachers come to know what an exceptionally well-behaved child and student you are then after you establish your great reputation then you can handle your own affairs but Lord knows it's hard to get rid of a bad rep after you get one so just look at Jonathan as your own personal bodyguard. Can you do that for me sir?"

"Yes, ma'am. But can I ask you a question ma'am."

"Absolutely."

"Why do you keep calling me sir?"

"For the same reason you keep calling me ma'am. It's just a term of endearment. It just means that you deserve my respect sir."

"Yeah, she calls everyone sir. It don't mean nothin'," Jason shot back. "It's better than when she calls you by your name. That usually means you're in big trouble. Like when she comes home from work and says Jason where are you. Then you know you're in big trouble. I usually know anyway that the principal's calling her 'cause I did something bad in school so 'sir's' cool with me."

Mama turned her head away from her youngest and smiled.

"C'mon and eat everyone. Dinner is served."

Cranberry waited 'til everyone was seated in their seats then took the lone seat that was open and stared at the table while everyone gave thanks and praise and took turns telling mama what happened in school and what they had for homework. Cranberry had never sat down to a real family dinner and was amazed at the food and people before him. He ate quietly choosing to simply take everything in and found himself smiling on several occasions usually around something the twins said. The two boys had to be put on separate sides of the table but still managed to kick each other when one got the better of the other. Jonathan played peacemaker while Mimi always seemed to be off in another world. Cranberry attributed this to her being a girl and ignored her for the most part as she did him.

When dinner was over and mama excused everyone each child got up and headed to a different area of the kitchen. Mimi cleared the table. Jonathan stood at the sink and rinsed all the dishes and put them in the dishwasher while Jason wiped the table and counters and set it for breakfast. And Jeremiah swept the floor and occasionally hit Jason with the broom when mama wasn't looking.

Cranberry was amazed at how disciplined and orderly everything was. Mama could see the boy's curiosity and explained it to Cranberry after dinner.

"I see you looking," she said smiling and patting the seat next to her. "These are my children Cranberry and the way I see it I'm responsible for them being on this earth so it's my job to make sure that they are fed and clothed and given everything needed so they can be successful and productive in life. So, I go to work every day to make sure they have everything it is that they need and the harder they work for themselves then the harder that I'll work for them. But that's not to say that they have a fee pass. They also owe me and themselves so they have chores to do since they don't work and put the food on the table.

They have two jobs. The first is to keep their house in order and to do well in school. And with the exception of Jeremiah they do this. Sometimes I believe that I picked up the wrong child with that one," she said glancing at Jeremiah who was now swinging the broom at his older sister. "Come here boy!" she screamed. Jeremiah walked over to her dropping his head sheepishly and waited for his mother to chastise him.

"What is wrong with you?" she said grabbing him and pulling him to her then tickling him until Jeremiah was nearly in tears. "Now you sit right here with me until they've finished their chores since you can't seem to work without antagonizing your brothers and sisters. Matter-of-fact bring me your homework while you're waiting so we can go over it."

"Ahh ma," Jeremiah said.

"Now."

"Anyway, I give and they give me back and for the most part it works out well. They can come to me at anytime and talk to me if they have something on their minds and I want you to feel free to do the same. I don't want you to feel any different. I've taken you into my home and consider you my child and will treat you as such so I'd appreciate you treating me as your mother if you see fit to do so. And with that said I also expect for you to put forth effort in school as well as at home. I want you to strive for greatness and if you fail we can still be satisfied with excellence. Just do your best Cranberry. Make me proud but most of all make yourself proud. Do you understand?"

Cranberry shook his head in agreement.

"Your chore starting tomorrow will be to vacuum and take the garbage out. Think you can handle that?"

Again the boy shook his head.

"I'm taking you down to school tomorrow and see if I can't get you enrolled. I have no paperwork—no birth certificate, shot record or anything—but we'll keep our fingers crossed and do our best. Now you go on and watch a little TV or ask the boys if it's okay if you play their Playstation. Ten o'clock it's lights out. Now come here and give me a hug Cranberry."

The boy was overcome with emotion as the woman squeezed him tightly.

"Thank you ma'am was all he could muster."

Ten minutes later when the big woman went into check on him she found him huddled up under the covers sound asleep.

The house was alive the next morning as Cranberry sat up and rubbed the sleep from his eyes.

"Need my Levi's yo. Gotta look fresh for the ladies and need my Tim's. Anybody seen my butter Tim's," shouted Jeremiah. "I laid 'em out right next to my Levi's. Okay who's the jokester. C'mon now I ain't got time. Y'all know I only wear my Tims when I got a test. Don't play! Mama!" Jeremiah screamed.

"What's with all the screamin' young man?"

"Mama ain't but one person can fit my Tims and you know they my good luck charm. I wear them whenever I have a test and Ms. Marshon giving us a test on the Civil War in social studies today."

"Did you study?"

"Yeah, I studied. You know I studied. You quizzed me last night."

"Yeah?"

"I meant yes ma'am."

"So you're prepared then."

"Yes ma'am. You know I'm ready ma."

"Then you don't need any shoes to give you good luck."

"Ah ma. You're right but you know I always wear my Tims whenever I have a test. Besides you tell us to lay our clothes out the night before and every time I do Jason acts like I'm layin' them out for him 'cause he don't ever take the time to lay his out. That's why he always looks like a bum."

"Is that any way to talk about your brother Jeremiah? Good morning Cranberry."

"Morning ma'am."

"Cranberry. Why in the hell would anybody name their kid cranberry?" Jeremiah said laughing hysterically before he hit the floor. Turning around and looking up the laughter gone Jeremiah was now on the verge of tears.

"I believe your brother warned you about your behavior last night. I'm thinking you should have heeded his advice. You don't insult my guests. Now get up and carry your little narrow behind to school."

"But ma…"

"Don't but ma me! Get your butt to school."

Jeremiah knew there was nothing else to say. He'd pushed the envelope and there was no changing mama's mind when she got like this.

"Did Jonathan lay your clothes out for you?"

"Yes, ma'am," Cranberry said looking at her somewhat differently now. He knew she loved Jeremiah but she hadn't thought twice about laying him out and he wondered if she would do the same to him if he got out of line. Well, if that's what happened when you got out of line he'd just make damn sure he'd never get out of line.

"Okay. Get dressed son. Give me twenty minutes and I'll be ready." Fifteen minutes later Cranberry, mama, Jonathan and a few of his friends made the short walk to Mother Cabrini. All went as well as could be and Cranberry found himself in a few of Jonathan's classes. When asked to stand up and introduce himself to the class there were a few snickers but Jonathan quickly put an end to that.

"Excuse me Ms. Martin. May I say something," Jonathan said.

"Yes, Jonathan."

"I just wanted to say Cranberry's my cousin and he's come to live with us and anybody that has a problem with Cranberry is going to have a problem with me. Hope that's understood. Thank you, Ms. Martin."

There was not another peep as Jonathan had long ago let it be known that he wasn't one to be played with. The rest of the day went pretty smoothly and when school was out the two boys met at the front of the school.

"You didn't have to do that, man."

"I know but like mama said you don't need to come there your first day and get in a fight and get a bad rep."

"I know but you know sooner or later somebody's gonna try me and I'm gonna have to handle it myself."

"I know and when that day comes just make sure you're off school grounds so they don't suspend you. It's better that way 'cause if you get suspended for fighting on school grounds then you really got problems. Then you gotta deal with mama and it's better to get in a fight and get whooped by some kid than to get a whoopin' by mama. Ya feel me."

"I feel ya," Cranberry said thinking of Jeremiah hitting the floor this morning. "Yeah, I guess you're right. I saw your mom beat Jeremiah this morning and it wasn't pretty."

"I'm tryna tell you."

The rest of the school year was pretty uneventful and Cranberry fell into the family flow rather easily. His own mother was now a distant memory and over the weeks he came to refer to the big woman as mama just like the rest of the clan. He and Jonathan were particularly close and seldom argued or disagreed on anything spending most of their time keeping Jason and Jeremiah in line although it was Jeremiah who garnered most of the attention. He wasn't bad just bright as hell and mischievous to boot with a mouth on him that would have made most sailors and dock workers envious.

One day walking home from school Jonathan and Cranberry noticed a large commotion up ahead and weren't real surprised to find Jeremiah in the midst of it.

Mother Cabrini had always made it a point to dismiss the children at different intervals so that the younger children wouldn't be in the same area as the older, bigger kids that way eliminating the smaller children from being picked on and being bullied yet here was Jeremiah in the middle of a group of sixth graders with the roles reversed. He was the one bullying and teasing them. This third grader was actually picking at a group of sixth graders.

"Least my mama don't gotta shit before I can eat," he said as Jonathan and Cranberry approached.

"You gotta lotta mouth kid. I wonder if you'd have all that mouth if you didn't have your big brother to come to your rescue every time."

"I don't need back up when it comes to your punk ass," he said spoiling for a fight.

"That's enough Jeremiah. And why aren't you home?" Jonathan said pushing his younger brother aside.

"I stopped at the video arcade. Mama said I could this morning."

"And I guess she gave you permission to start a fight on the way home from the arcade too?"

Jeremiah stood there not backing down from Jonathan or the other boys.

"And you think all your mouth is gonna help you beat Raffy and his boys?"

"I can beat Raffy's punk ass on my worst day," Jeremiah said knowing that Jonathan would at least not let them jump him.

"Is that right? Well, today you're gonna get your chance to see and may the best man win 'cause I'm out. Don't beat him too bad Raffy," Jonathan said before walking away.

Jeremiah was shocked but didn't back down.

"C'mon punk ass. What?! You think I need my brother to beat your ass?"

Cranberry who had been this route before only to watch as Jonathan would invariably snatch Jeremiah up and take him home was shocked.

"Hey J. You can't leave the kid out there like that. You know Raffy and his boys are punks just like Jeremiah said. You know they ain't gonna fight him straight up on account that there's a good chance that Jeremiah will beat his ass even though he's only in the third grade and littler than him."

"I know but Jeremiah's gotta learn you can't go around tryin' to take on the world."

"C'mon J. He's just a kid."

"He's gotta learn."

"Not today he won't," Cranberry said turning and racing back down the street toward the fight. The crowd had grown doubling in size and the two were hard at it with

Jeremiah backing the tough talk up and getting the best of the bigger boy raining down punches and bloodying Raffy's nose even more with each blow. Cranberry loved the boy and all his energy. He knew Jeremiah would take on the world if he felt he'd been wronged and was doing so now with all the effort and skill of a Samurai warrior when Raffy's boys decided enough was enough.

Picking up a small pipe one of them approached Jeremiah from the back. Before he could strike Jeremiah with the pole Cranberry hit him with a bolo shot that sent the boy reeling. Two or three others came running to their boys defense and Cranberry swiftly sidestepped the first boy and sent a thundering left hook to the boy's solar plexus that left him gasping for air. The second boy who obviously thought Cranberry's first punch was a lucky punch joined right in the melee only to have Cranberry put a move on him that sent him sprawling and laid him flat out on the ground just like the first. By this time Jeremiah and Raffy were sitting up staring in awe as a third boy joined the fracas only to meet the same fate as the first two.

The crowd stood by in amazement as Cranberry snatched Jeremiah up by the collar and walked over to meet Jonathan who was equally stunned by what he had just witnessed.

"Oh my God! Did you see that J.? C. took on three of them and ain't got a scratch. I mean he…"

"I saw Jeremiah. And I tell you I ain't never seen nothing like that. Where'd you learn to fight like that?"

Cranberry dropped his head in embarrassment.

"My dad was a fighter. He used to make me go to the gym with him every day."

"Wow! Why didn't you say anything?"

"I don't know. I just never liked fighting. At my old school I used to fight everyday because kids used to tease me about my name and my mom."

"I can understand about your name but what did your moms do?"

"Chill, Jeremiah. You run your mouth too much. That's why you almost got your ass kicked. Always running your mouth. When C. gets ready to tell you he will. Now chill and clean yourself up so mama don't go thinkin' you got into some shit again."

Jeremiah ignored his older brother and turned to Cranberry who was now a hero in the young boy's eyes.

"Yo, C. you think you can teach me how to fight like that?"

Cranberry smiled.

"Half a Harlem would be in Harlem Hospital," Jonathan joked.

"Maybe when you're older," Cranberry answered laughing with Jonathan.

"Now no mention of this to mama you two. She's got enough on her plate not to have to worry about her kids fighting out here in these streets."

"Ain't gotta worry about me. I ain't tryna get beat twice in a day. They may not be able to beat me out here but that woman's got a heavy hand. She hits like a man. Come to think about it she looks like one too." Jeremiah said laughing at his own joke.

"There you go again," Jonathan said chasing him through the courtyard.

"Let me go first. You two slide on into your rooms and change clothes before she notices anything?"

Mama was in her room when the three boys came in. Jeremiah and Cranberry headed straight to their rooms and changed clothes. Jonathan knocked on his mother's bedroom door.

"It's me ma. Just letting you know we're home."

"You seen Jeremiah. I told him he could go to the video arcade on his way home from school but he should have been home by now. I told him to be home by five."

"He's here ma. He's in his room changing his clothes."

"Oh, okay. That boy worries me."

"Don't let him ma. He's a good kid."

"Yeah, I guess it could be worse. You know Ms. Levy's son is the same age as Jeremiah and he's out there pushing that stuff."

"I know ma. You don't have to worry about Jeremiah ma. He's a good kid."

"Tell him I want to see him. He worries me."

"I'll do that ma."

Minutes later there was another knock at mama's door.

"Who is it?"

"It's me ma. Jeremiah."

"Do me a favor and go help Mimi set the table for dinner."

"Oh okay. I thought you wanted me for something."

"No, what you thought was you were in trouble. And why is that Jeremiah?"

The boy smiled sheepishly. He was only too glad mama couldn't see him. She had a way of reading his face making it almost impossible to lie to her.

"I didn't think that at all. Ask anyone and they'll tell you Jeremiah Ball is a wonderful child and the only that doesn't think so is his big, ol, mean ol, bear of a mother," he said doubling over with laughter.

He could hear her heavy footsteps coming towards the door and let out a shriek and headed for the front door. Jonathan, Jason and Cranberry were doubled over as well but did their best to hide their laughter when mama came out of her room. Jeremiah's remarks were too funny and the next thing they knew they were rolling again. By this time Mimi had made her way into the living room.

"Anybody gonna let me in on the joke?"

Jason repeated it and Mimi was soon clutching her sides as well.

"No, he didn't call you a mean ol' bear," she laughed.

"And you're going to repeat that little heathen's remarks!"

"Don't get mad at me ma. I didn't say it," Mimi laughed. "Where is he? I gotta give him a pound on that one."

"Look at you encouraging that little devil. He's out in the hall scared for his life. Go get him and tell him to get in here and set the table like I asked him to."

Jeremiah came to the door a grin still spread wide against his chocolate stained cheeks.

"Get in here outta that hall boy with all that hoopin' and hollerin'," the woman said. There was no laughter on her face although little did they know she was smiling inside.

"Ah ma. Don't be mad. I was just teasin' you," Jeremiah sad easin' into the house.

"You know if I had ever made a comment like that to my mother I would have still been picking my teeth up off the floor."

"And that's why I have you as my mother instead of that wicked ol' witch," he said inadvertently.

"Oh so now it's not bad enough you insulted me now you're talking about my mother," she said getting up and trapping the young boy in a corner of the kitchen.

Grabbing him she pulled him tightly to her and began tickling him and mashing him into the kitchen cabinet. The boy was laughing hysterically and could barely catch his breath. When he did he shouted loud enough for the neighbors to hear.

"Stop it ma! You're smothering me. You big bear," Jeremiah screamed before falling to the floor in fits of laughter.

Cranberry and the others stood laughing almost as hard as Jeremiah.

"Come on my loves. It's time to eat. The mood was warm and pleasant as the children took their usual places around the table.

"How did your test go without your Tims Jeremiah?"

"I'm pretty sure I aced it."

"That's good. Anything else happen today that you'd like to share?"

Jeremiah's head immediately turned to Cranberry and then to Jonathan who gave him a shut up or else look.

Call it women's intuition but they seemed to always know when something wasn't right or things were being held back and mama was no different.

"What is it Jeremiah?"

"Nothing ma," he said fearing his older brother almost as much as he did his mother. Knowing the results would be the same should she ask her eldest she turned to Cranberry.

"What are they not telling me sir?"

Cranberry who had not learned to withhold information from mama dropped his head.

"Nothing ma'am."

"I can look at you young man and tell that there is something you're not telling me and I'm waiting for an explanation and I'm not going to wait much longer."

"Well, ma Jonathan and I were walking home…"

Cranberry recounted the whole story much as it had happened and when he'd finished Jeremiah had all he could do not to knock over his kool-aid.

"Calm down Jeremiah."

"But ma you should have been there. C. can really fight. It's like he knows the art of war. I mean he's got moves like on TV. Those boys didn't know what hit them," he said jumping up from the table trying to duplicate C.'s moves and resembling a miniature Bruce Lee.

"Ma you should have seen it," Jeremiah squealed elated at being able to retell the story.

"It was really something to see, ma," Jonathan was forced to add with a smile.

"Dag! And I missed it," Jason said remorsefully.

"Jeremiah was beating one of the kids in my class pretty good so three of his friends tried to jump Jeremiah and in like five minutes Cranberry took care of all three and they never laid a hand on him. Honestly ma, I have never seen anybody better with their hands. You should have seen him."

The older woman was shocked by the news and it took a few minutes for her to gather herself. It was great that Jeremiah had come home in one piece. There had been days when she had to hold her youngest and console him while patching up his dings and bruises. That had been a long time ago before he'd learn to get good with his hands. Now there was little to worry about other than whether Jeremiah had a reason for being in the fight. Still, fighting was nothing that she condoned and she'd always taught her children that although it was much harder to walk away that was the Christian thing to do. Jeremiah, however, was never inclined to be very religious.

"Well, the boys both seem to be very impressed with your fighting skills Cranberry. You know I don't approve of fighting but under the circumstances I think you did the admirable thing in coming to Jeremiah's defense. And I don't blame you. Who I blame is Jeremiah who seems unable to stay out of fights. My youngest here has never seen a bad fight or a fight he didn't like. But tell me. How did you come to acquire your fighting prowess?"

"Ma'am?"

"How did you get to be so good with your hands?"

Cranberry had everyone's attention.

"My dad was a fighter and used to take me to the gym everyday and so I studied the mixed martial arts from the time I was about five til last year when he went away to the war."

"And you haven't seen him since?"

"No, ma'am. My mom got a telegram one day saying he was killed in Fallujah and then she—uhm—well, she was never the same. And then one day she just left and never came back. I guess I was out in the streets for about a year when you picked me up," Cranberry said reaching for the meatloaf.

It was the first time Cranberry had ever spoken of himself and his former life and you could hear a pin drop.

"So, you enjoy fighting?"

"No ma'am. I mean I don't like beating up people. I enjoyed training and making my dad proud of me. I enjoyed competing against older kids and winning my competitions but I don't enjoy fighting and beating people up or causing them pain. Besides my dad used to always say if you can beat someone and do it then you're a punk. And most of the kids I'm pretty sure I can beat so I just walk away."

"Do you fight a lot?"

"C'mon Jeremiah. How long have I been here?"

Jeremiah sat back and thought.

"Exactly! And how many times have you seen me get in a fight?"

"Today was the first time," Jeremiah said smiling at his new found hero.

"Precisely! And if it wasn't for you I still wouldn't have gotten into a fight."

"So, why do you let those kids pick on you about your name?"

"Ah, they ain't doin' nothin' but having fun. And with a name like Cranberry what do you expect? But they don't mean no harm. Besides I was taught the martial arts as a way to harness my energies and show discipline not to inflict pain."

"So, son how good were you?"

"I think I was pretty good ma'am. When I was nine I used to compete in the thirteen year old bracket and I had a 32-0 record. I guess I was pretty good."

"And you just let it go?"

Cranberry smiled.

"When my ma left I think I was more interested in eating than fighting and competing," he said reaching for more mashed potatoes.

"And it appears little has changed," mama said smiling. "I'm glad you shared that with us Cranberry. There's a dojo not far from here run by an old friend of mine. Tomorrow after work I'm going to see if I can't get you and Jeremiah enrolled. I don't think you should give up on something you're good at and hopefully it will give Jeremiah the same discipline and use up some of his excess energy."

"Ah ma, I want to go too," Jason shouted.

"We'll see sweetheart."

"Thanks ma," Cranberry said. "But I was wondering if I could apply for that job at Mr. Ortiz's bodega. I talk to him every day after school and he was telling me that he needs someone to stock the shelves and make deliveries right here in the neighborhood."

"Let me think about that son but if you don't mind me asking why do you want to go to work at so early an age? Don't you know that you'll be working the rest of your life?"

"No disrespect ma but why does anyone go to work? I mean Mimi has a part-time job and you know what the difference between her and me is?"

Mimi's head popped up.

"Oh, I can't wait to hear this one," Mimi chirped in.

"The difference between Mimi and me is she always looks fresh."

"Oh, so that's it. Kids are picking at you at school?"

"Well, yeah sort of. They say things like, 'Yo C. I like that shirt man. Liked it even better last year when J. had it on.'"

Jeremiah fell out of his chair laughing.

"Oh dip! That's a good one. I gotta use that one tomorrow," he laughed.

"So, that's what it is. I forgot how mean kids can be but I'd much rather you concentrate on your school work and your martial arts. Those two can take you somewhere but working for Mr. Ortiz—and don't get me wrong Mr. Ortiz is a good man—but there's no future in it."

"I'm not trying to be ungrateful or anything. I mean J.'s hand-me-downs are cool and everything but they're J.'s flavor not mine and I just want some gear that says this is me, Cranberry."

"I understand son. I usually do school shopping twice a year—once at the beginning of the year and then right around now when I get my income tax back. You just missed that but let me see what I have left in the bank. You meet me at Macy's on 34th when you get out of school and we'll see if we can't pick you up a few things but that's with your word that you'll keep making good grades. The minute I see your grades slipping I'll come to school and strip you. I'm paying for grades. You understand?"

"And she'll do it to," Jeremiah said still smiling. "I remember when Ms. Hodge called mama when I was in second grade. I had this nice sheepskin coat and it was right before Christmas break and Ms. Hodge, that old witch, called mama and told her that my behavior wasn't too good and my grades were slipping and the next thing I knew mama was outside my classroom. She pulled me out of class and beat me right then and there in front of my whole class then told me to get my coat and hat. I had the hat to match and she said since I didn't want to do anything but act the fool at school then there was no need for me to go anymore. She made me walk home with no hat or coat and it was December. I damn near froze. I was gonna call protective services but she wouldn't let me use her cell to call on her. She said she wasn't paying me to go to school to act like no fool. Then when we got home she made me scrub the bathroom and vacuum the whole house. Said without school all I was going to end up as was a janitor. I had to stay home like three days just cleaning and scrubbing. Trust me. I ain't never get in no more trouble in school."

Mama put her head down to keep the children from seeing her smile.

"I ain't lyin' either am I Jason?"

"Nope. Mama don't play when it comes to us getting' our education."

"She's always saying it's the key to our future and the only way to unlock the possibilities," Mimi added.

"So, do we have a deal young man?"

"And on the way back from Macy's we'll stop at the dojo. Remind me to leave carfare for you and Jeremiah on the counter in the morning. I'm going to be gone early so I can get off early and take you two."

"Yes ma'am."

"You should get some of those butter wheat Tims Berry. Then me and you will be the only ones at school with a pair." Jeremiah said. "Then everyone will know we're brothers for sure."

"I was sorta leanin' towards a pair of those Nike Air Max Goadome's and a couple of pair of Levi's."

"Ah man Nike's are whacked."

"They're not whacked Jeremiah. They're just not your flavor," Jonathan shot back.

"What do you know?! All your taste is in your mouth J." Jeremiah said grinning.

"That's enough you two. Tell me about your day Jason."

That night Cranberry went to sleep in a warm bed with his new family led by a woman who truly loved and cared about him. And tomorrow she was taking him clothes shopping. Cranberry Brown was happier than he'd been in a long time.

The months went by and soon turned into years. Mimi was now in her second year at Rutger's and Jonathan and Cranberry were finishing up there last year at DeWitt Clinton High School. Honor roll students both planned on staying near home to look after mama and the boys. Jonathan was in the midst of receiving academic, track and basketball, scholarships from a variety of schools but both he and Cranberry had limited their options to Columbia and N.Y.U. and mama couldn't have been happier with their choices.

"Two of the finest boys a mother could ever ask for," she would say regularly as she hugged her two giants. Jonathan now stood six four in his stocking feet and Cranberry wasn't far behind at six two.

Neither had changed much. Sure they'd matured. Cranberry went on to stack up so many wrestling and martial arts trophy's that mama was forced to get a separate storage unit just to store them. And Jonathan wasn't far behind. Cranberry even had a girlfriend who mama considered her second daughter she was around so much. Even Jeremiah had calmed down some and after six years of working out at the dojo alongside of Cranberry no longer saw fighting as a means to an end. And Jason was well—Jason—

still quiet and introspective and the child mama considered closest to who she was. All were doing well and mama beamed with pride.

Oh, there had been challenges. Like when Cranberry's mother arrived out of the blue, all highed up and demanding that her son come back home and live with her when he was sixteen or seventeen.

Cranberry was speechless as he watched his family come to his defense.

At first, the woman appeared pleasant and congenial suggesting the person she may have been at an earlier time in her life but after meeting with considerable opposition from those that had over the years come to love him she began to lose it and the years in the clutches of her drug use on the streets, and in The Tombs finally began to show itself.

"I want my son and if you people don't give him to me now I'll go and get the law and charge all your asses for kidnapping," the woman shouted at the only two who were home at the time.

It was then—in the middle of her tirade—that mama along with Cranberry, Jeremiah and Jonathan walked in. Cranberry recognized his mother right away. What child doesn't recognize his own mother but he did not know this woman that had given him birth.

"Ah baby it's been so long. I walked out the door that day and was mistakenly identified and falsely arrested. I spent eight years in lock up for a crime I didn't commit and all I thought of was you," she said the tears dripping down her face. "I've been out for two days and haven't slept a wink. All I've been doing is looking for my baby. I searched everywhere until I ran into Ms. Levy who told me that she used to feed you until this good woman picked you up and took you home with her. C'mon baby. Get your things. We're going home."

Cranberry didn't move.

"C'mon boy! I said we're going home."

To everyone's surprise it was Mimi who spoke first.

"Miss Brown Cranberry isn't going anywhere. He is home."

"Yes ma'am. We've made a nice home here for Cranberry and you're not just going to waltz in here after eight years and demand that he leave his family—the only family he knows—and go traipsing off into the unknown.," Jason added.

"Now you wait one minute young man. Cranberry is my son and I demand that you give him to me. Get your clothes son."

"The only reason you want Cranberry is because you're looking for a meal ticket. If you cared anything about him you wouldn't have left a seven year old home alone to go get some drugs. And the only reason you want him now is so you can get a check from social services so you can keep shooting that shit in your veins. Well, he ain't

going nowhere with you," Jason said standing and screaming at the woman in front of

him. "You damn junkie. How long were you out before you ran to get some more of that

shit? And you think you're going to throw my boy into that ol' crazy shit? I'm telling

you right now it ain't happening!"

"Jason!" Mama screamed. "Is that any way to talk to an adult?"

"You know he's right mama," Mimi countered. "She ain't taking Cranberry

nowhere."

"I'm tryna tell you," Jonathan added.

"Well, like I said I'll get the law and charge your fat ass with kidnappin'," she

said looking at mama.

And right then and there something clicked within Cranberry and as he started to

rise and move towards the woman it was Jonathan who grabbed him and held him.

"And what law is going to give custody to a woman, a drug addict who does eight

years in jail and abandons her seven year old child. You'd better get a grip," Mimi

countered. "And if you say something else about my mother I'm gonna forget my mama

teachin' me to be a Christian and beat your ass 'til you wish you were back in jail. Now

you get your ass up and get the fuck outta my house."

"Mimi!" mama yelled. "I will not tolerate that kind of language in my house."

Funny thing though. The person who loved Cranberry perhaps more than anyone else in the family sat there speechless.

"Hey ma."

"Yes, Jeremiah."

"Ma'am. All a y'all fightin' over who gets Cranberry and where he's gonna go. And ain't nobody askin' him what he wants to do."

"You're absolutely right," mama said in agreement. Will you abide by your son's choice ma'am?"

The woman looked down at her shoes knowing that she had little choice. He was old enough now that she couldn't force him to stay with her. If he chose to go home with her it would be of his own volition and so she was forced to agree.

"Cranberry, I think it's time we go home son."

There was a pause as everyone in the room sat awaiting his reply with bated breath.

"I am home ma," he said.

When she was gone each one of his siblings came over and hugged him.

"Nice to have you back home again son," mama said hugging today's favorite son.

"I never left mama."

Achua the Boy Prophet

I hated massa. Sometimes after he would leave my hut I would cry myself to sleep. With all the gals on the place why did he choose me? There were a whole lot that were much more purtier than me but he always chose me. I hated those nights when he would just come walking in too drunk to stand up and fall on me smelling all musty and stank and likkered up and rip my clothes off. And to this day I cain't unnerstand why he pick me. Like I said there was a lot purtier girls in the quarters than me.

I was twelve when he first came and the apple of my daddy's eye. And daddy hardly paid me any mine no more. Daddy acted like it was my fault and all but disowned me. And I hated daddy for not killing that evil white man for deflowering me. By the time I was thirteen I was pregnant with Achua my first born. I named him after my grandfather back in Africa but massa said he was to be called John after him.

And despite the way Achus was conceived I loved that boy and so did mama. I really think daddy did too but he wasn't one to show emotion so it was hard to tell.

Funny thing was with all massa's slaves he had a certain fondness for Achua too. That's

not to say that he has a certain fondness for anyone. Massa Jennings didn't like nary a

soul white or niggra. Massa was a large mountain of a man with an evil disposition no

matta where he went. Most folks would see him coming and get out of his way and pray

that he won't come a lookin' for them. He didn't associate with anyone and when he did

it was never on good terms. Mama said he had the devil in him. So when I found out I

was carrying his child I prayed that God would take this child but I suppose the good

Lord knew better ad nine months later he sent me a beautiful baby boy.

Achua had one affliction however and that was that one leg was noticeably

shorter than the other but daddy said I should be grateful that was all that was wrong with

him considering all the afflictions his daddy had. We laughed at that for a long time.

As Achua blossomed into a beautiful little boy I was surprised to find that I was

not the only one that loved my little boy. Everyone seemed to have a fondness for

Achua even massa who took the little boy everywhere he went. When massa went

fishing he'd come to get Achua. When massa went deer hunting he'd come to get Achua.

Folks said when he'd talk to Achua that's the only time they'd see him smile. Mama said

massa truly loved Achua but daddy saw things from a whole different view. He said that

Jesus and the devil had found a common ground. But he was only afraid of the devil

influencing my little angel. Me and mama didn't see this as funny.

When Achua was seven or eight years old most of the people started calling

Achua 'Man' on account of him having such an old spirit. Others said he was destined and still others said he was a prophet on account of when he spoke people young and old would gather to listen. To me he was just my baby boy.

By the time he was thirteen or fourteen I began to realize that there was something different, something special about Achua aside from the fact that one leg was shorter and he walked with a noticeable limp but mama was quick to point out that where there is a shortcoming the Lord makes up for those shortcomings with other blessings.

I one was one of the one's that truly believed this as Achua was wise beyond his years. It was not long after that that Achua stood up in one of our Sunday gatherings not long after the preacher died and gave a most stirring speech on Moses leading the Israelites out of Egypt. So aroused was the congregation of slaves that they ordained Achua the prophet almost in the same vein as they did Moses and vowed patience as he suggested and truly believed that Achua would lead them out of their own bondage.

Not long after Achua was named the preacher something unheard of for a fourteen year old and he assumed the position and did an admirable job as people from neighboring plantations came to hear the young boy prophesize on the upcoming exodus.

It was only a matter of time before massa got wind of these gatherings and came to speak to me concerning Achua's growing popularity.

"Mary I hear that John has taken over for Cicero and has been named the new preacher."

"Yassuh massa. That be correct."

"And from what I hear he's very good and commands quite a crowd. They say that he even has niggras from miles around travelling to hear him speak on Sunday mornings?"

"I never ast where the folks come from massa. I just goes to hear the Word of God from Achua's mouth."

"I keep telling you the boy's name is Johnny," massa said drawing back his hand to backhand me.

Achua's timing couldn't have been better as he walked into the cabin.

"Mama, Massa John," he said as he grabbed a seat on the empty wooden rum cask.

"I'm good John. I was just talking to your mama about you taking over Cicero's place and your preaching the Word of God. I didn't know you were so religious. Do you mind telling me what so inspired you to take on such a calling?"

"Why no 'suh. It was you 'suh. I remember when you used to call us all together on Sunday mornin's and preach the gospel and ever since then I knew that's what I wanted to do."

Massa Jennings couldn't help but smile but it was short lived.

"Preaching the Word of God can be quite fulfilling as long as you don't distort his word. I've been hearing from a few of the other plantation owners that a good many of their niggras have been coming to hear you speak and are coming back saying things like our God is a jealous God and you can only serve one master. Did you say that?"

"That's what you told us."

Again Massa Jennings dropped his head to prevent us from seeing him smile..

"I understand son but with the recent uprisings in Southampton where Nat Turner posing as a preacher and got seventy of his followers to follow him on what was supposed to be a message from God these folks are uneasy 'bout you preachin' to their niggras."

"But I ain't ast them to come massa. They just show up."

"Understood. But I'm suspending all Sunday services until the panic dies down. Do you understand? There will be no more preaching, holding church services or bible studies until you hear from me. Is that understood?"

"Yassuh massa suh."

"Now c'mon grab your fishing gear. Fish should be bitin' good this time of morning."

"Would it be okay if I didn't go today 'suh. Mama's been strugglin' right through here."

"Step outside John and let me have a quick word with your mama."

"Yassuh massa suh."

As soon as the door was shut the massuh set in on me like there was no tomorrow and I was the one responsible for the world coming to an end.

"Woman, what is wrong with you now? That boy looks after you like he's the daddy and you're the child instead of you lookin' after him. And every time I turn around somethin's ailin' you. What the hell is it now?"

"I think I'm with child massuh," I said clutching my stomach and head. "I haven't told the boy but it's getting harder and harder to lift things around here."

And for the first time in a long time massa was speechless. I guess he realized it was his as he forbid me from seeing or being with anyone else. Not that he had to. I had no hankering to be with him or any other man. To me and thanks to him I loathed lying down with anyone.

"Well, you keep it to yourself. The missus is already putting me through hell for my being so close to John. She says he bears too much of a likeness to me and says she's going to do away with him and the wench that bore him soon as she finds out who it is. So, let's just keep this between us. And if I were you I would get to cozying up with one of these young bucks just so's you has an alibi if she comes snoopin' around. Don't help none that she can't bear me any children."

"Yassuh massa."

Little did I know that Achua was standing at the door listenin'. I'd never let on that massa was his daddy and never had he asked but now that he knew his whole temperament changed.

That day he stayed to help me with the laundry and croppin' tobacco but every mother knows her child and there was something different about my son that day. He was unusually quiet and from that day on he grew apart just as my daddy had done when he learned that the massa had taken me for his wench.

Achua now preferred spending more and more time with his grandfather and his questions tended to be more and more of a serious nature than they'd been in the past," I attributed this to his becoming a man but his grandfather and grandmother saw something different.

"Achua has become angry and bitter," my mother commented.

"And rightly so. He sees the irony of this slave master who on Sunday would preach the gospel of Jesus as being the same man who raped his mother and impregnated her as a child and considers us as no more than farm animals to be used. He is not only angry. He is bitter."

"And you see this as being good my husband?"

"I never said I saw it as being good. I just said I understand how the boy feels," papa said.

"Can you imagine what white folks are feeling after Nat Turner, who called himself a preacher killed fifty six innocent white folks including women and children for no apparent reason."

"Woman, the same man that has shackled us and put us in chains is the same man that took your daughter and raped and impregnated her at the age of twelve. He's the same man that gets rich off of our labor and you dare say to me that what Nat Turner did in retaliation for this treatment was for no apparent reason. Woman don't even address me in that manner as if Nat Turner was at fault. You make me think that I am a fool for choosing you to be my wife."

"I'm not saying he didn't have good reason husband. But you have t unnerstand massa's fear my husband."

"Sho I unnerstand his fear. His fear is that niggras will rise up and finally make him accountable for the pain and suffering he has caused us."

"And you see this as being right as good Christians?"

"I have a long time ago forgotten about right and wrong. But I know what is just. And the Holy Koran that what is just is an eye-for-an-eye. You cannot rape a man's daughter and not expect a man to retaliate. If he does not how can he call himself a man?"

"What are you telling me my husband? That you have forgotten your Christian teachings and not learned to turn the other cheek?"

"I am Yoruba, my wife and a Yoruba warrior is taught early on to protect his family but I don't suspect that you have to be Muslim or Yoruba to know or believe that. I believe Massa Jennings who has no religion affiliations or beliefs but to enslave believes that same doctrine which is why he doesn't want Achua to preach. He is protecting what is his and that is his family and his way of life as he knows it. Why woman should I not do the same for my loved ones. If your Jesus tells me not to do this then I must turn to a god that knows my sorrow and my grief and who expects me to seek retribution and justice."

"And this is what you teach your grandson who grows more bitter every day?"

"No woman. What I teach my grandson is to be a man, to be aware and to know injustice. What I seek to teach my grandson is that a man who stands for nor nothing will fall for anything. What I teach my grandson is that he should be a far stronger man than his grandfather and to strike out when he sees the brutality and cruelty of this institution they call slavery. What I teach my grandson is to be ready to die in the fight against much in the same way Nat Turner did."

My mother began to weep.

"And you know you are setting him up to be an angry young man. He is already bitter and the boy has a gift. He is a leader of men—some say a prophet—but where will he lead those that follow being so bitter and calloused?"

"Perhaps he will lead the children of Israel out of the pharaohs clutches. Perhaps he will lead the exodus."

"Or die."

"Or die," papa admonished.

When they were finished we were all crying—well that is except Achua—who stood their stoically.

It was Saturday evening and when we left my parent's cabin I repeated massas words to Achua who said he had heard massa when it came to suspending church service. But on Sunday morning he was up with the roosters.

"Where are you going?" I asked as he dressed in his Sunday clothes.

"Why mother I have but one master and it is my duty to serve him."

Who was I to disagree? Dressing quickly I followed and was surprised to find a larger group than usual gathered for services.

Taking the pulpit which consisted of a large wooden box Achua addressed the gathering.

"As I'm sure you know we have been forbidden to gather here today and I'm sure we will be punished severely or at least I will be for disobeying massa's command but I want y'all to know I serve but one master and he is a jealous god. And I have been called to spread His word and His word alone and so I stand before you as did David before Goliath and as did Moses before the pharaohs telling you that our time is now. Not tomorrow! But we must begin our exodus from this bondage and no man who calls himself massa shall oversee The Lord Jesus Christ. We serve but one god and His name is the Lord Jesus Christ. So go now and pack your meager belongings. Our journey begins tonight. We will seek the Promised Land and whoever stands in our way will encounter the wrath of the Lord."

And with that Achua stepped down from the pulpit and walked away. The crowd stood there in disbelief and then slowly they approached me and asked. 'what time are we supposed to meet Sister Mary?' I was as surprised as they were and not knowing I simply said seven o'clock as that was when dusk fell. I then turned and followed Achua.

Once home I approached my son.

"Son, do you really mean to go through with this?"

"I do mother. It is God's work and I believe that it is time."

"And you are sure you are not simply reacting to massa and your grandfather?"

"You mean my father and my grandfather? If that's what you are asking me then yes I am reacting to both with God the Father as my guide. Both men make claims that they have my best interest at heart. If I had continued preaching Exodus this is where it would have taken me. And massa knows that. The word would have eventually gotten back to the other plantation owners and they would have been forced to make massa contend with me and as I am do the Lord's work and would have continued he would have been forced to kill me. Massa Jennings loves me as a son whether he knows it or not but he forbade me to hold services. Being that this was the last time I will have them all in one place it was abrupt but it is time. My grandfather only went so far as to reinforce the plight of my people and exhort me to carry out His plan for the exodus."

"They ast me what time you want them to meet? And I told them dusk."

"Will you be joining us mother?"

"Do I have a choice? Massa already told me that I was no mother."

"You are all the mother a boy could ask for."

I immediately began gathering my things for our journey. When I finished I went to my parent's cabin to bid them farewell only to find that they were already packed and waiting to leave. To me everything seemed too awfully abrupt and piecemeal but it seemed after making my rounds to say goodbye that everyone was packed and had been well-schooled in what was to take place but me. On returning to our cabin I ast Achua how it was that everyone seemed so calm and reserved almost as if this had been in the works for some time.

"It has mama. Everyone has been waiting for this day but I could not tell you as massa may have beaten you or somehow coerced you into telling him what we were plotting. So, at the risk of all the others I had to conceal our plans from you until now. I was only trying to protect you mama."

"And so, my son you feel that at your age you are ready for so large an undertaking?"

"Yes mother. You see we have the one thing on our side that will prevail against all odds?"

"I don't know how you can think that. I just made the rounds thinking I was saying goodbye and I may have seen five rifles in good working order."

"That is hardly the one thing that will prevail against all odds mama."

"What do you have then? Is there something I don't know?"

"Yes, mama. We have the Lord Jesus Christ to guide us."

"I'm in no way trying to dissuade you my son but the Lord Jesus may be all powerful up there but white folks like massa got guns down here. And soon as they get wind of this here exodus they gonna string you up to the closest tree."

Showing no fear Achua smiled at me.

"Grab your thangs mama. It's just about that time. And would you tell grandpa that we're ready."

Leaving the cabin I noticed a great many of the slaves walking towards the big house which surprised me as well. You would have thought that they would have been trying to sneak away quietly. But no they all carried small satchels and headed to the big house almost as if they were going to say farewell to massa. It all seemed to be a part of a dream and I was forced to pinch myself to make sure that it was not.

Upon reaching my parent's cabin mama let me know that daddy was already on his way. Even more confused I helped her with her belongings and we too joined the long procession and headed towards the big house.

Achua soon joined us and walked to the front of the ever increasing group of slaves which had to number close to two hundred now.

Walking up to the front porch he shouted. The rest of us stood not more than ten feet behind him on the fringes of the apple orchard.

"Massa Jennings," he shouted. "Massa Jennings!"

The tall bulky white man known to most of us as massa appeared on the front door naked to the waist.

"What is it boy? What's happened?"

"Nothing's happened massa."

"Then why are all you niggras gathered here? If it's about the Sunday services they have been suspended until further notices. I thought I made that clear."

"No suh. This isn't about that at all. This is about us proclaiming ourselves free and letting you know that we are at this very moment leaving this here den of inequity. We can only serve one massa and that massa that we choose to serve goes by the name of Jesus Christ not John Jennings."

I must admit I have never been so proud of my son. I longed for the day I would stand up to this white man and could look him in the eye and say no more but I'd never come to overcome my fear yet here was my fifteen year old son doing just that.

"Why you ungrateful…"

Massa never got a chance to finish his sentence or take that next step as a rifle shot from right over our heads in the apple orchard caught massa in the thigh and sent him rolling down the porch steps in agonizing pain.

"You ungrateful 'lil bastard. You shot me."

"No. I shot you you heathen white man. You who whipped, beat, and raped my daughter when she was twelve—this was long overdue—you do not deserve to live," my grandfather said his tears now flowing in anger. "The truth is I should have killed you a long time ago."

"Why nigga I'll have you whipped and hanged for this. Buck, Esau grab this crazy nigga but there was no movement from either until my grandfather nodded at which time Buck and Esau grbbed massa and dragged him towards the barn.

"Sista Ophelia!"

"Yes Achua."

"You know where he keeps his papers and money. Make out a writ stating that I Massa John Jenning on this 4th day of April in the year of our Lord 1831 emancipate my slaves and afford them safe passage north from Virginia to Delaware where they are to meet with one Hans Lofgren."

"Yes Achua. But Massa Jennings keeps his money in a safe in the study that he keeps locked."

"Go to my grandfather then and get the combination."

They'd already dragged massa into the barn and from the screams I feared it might be too late but after another shotgun blast Ophelia came back all smiles.

"He was only too glad to give it up," she said the smile ever present.

Once the money and paperwork were in order I sent the hundred or so followers on their way and went to check on my grandfather. Entering the barn I found massa hanging upside down from one of the butchering cables. Mama had doubled back too and was talking to massa as my grandfather, Buck and Esau sat there just to insure her safety.

And mama took her time remembering each time massa had entered her cabin in the wee hours of the morning in a drunken stupor and raped her or beaten her for not performing some ungodly act in the manner he proposed. With my grandfather's razor she made long incisions running the length of massas penis until he passed out from the pain. And each time he would pass out either Buck or my grandfather would throw a bucket of cold water on him to revive him at which time mama would begin carving into his flesh again until there were strips of massa's penis hang free.

"I guess we're all done here. He should bleed out by morning," Buck said.

"Not quite yet," mama said gathering the whip and striking him; each blow tearing deep into the skin of his back.

When his back was completely raw and she was exhausted from whipping him it was she who brought the bucket of cold water and revived him this time. Once she had revived him she went to the sack of salt grabbed fistfuls and rubbed it into both his back and genitals. The pain must have been excruciating as I have never heard a man make such spine chilling screams for mercy. The more he begged for mama to show him mercy the more salt mama would get to rub into his open wounds until Buck had to pull her away and insist that he had enough.

We reached the rest of the group midway through the night and by dawn we had reached the Delaware River and safe passage. Free at last! Free at last! Thank God almighty. I'm free at last!

amazon
3/7/16
19.99

Made in the USA
San Bernardino, CA
25 February 2016